Introduction to SDGs

Goals for a Better Planet

by Haruyo Yamaguchi
Ed Jacob

Level 4
(2000-word)

JN086662

IBC パブリッシング

はじめに

　ラダーシリーズは、「はしご（ladder）」を使って一歩一歩上を目指すように、学習者の実力に合わせ、無理なくステップアップできるよう開発された英文リーダーのシリーズです。

　リーディング力をつけるためには、繰り返したくさん読むこと、いわゆる「多読」がもっとも効果的な学習法であると言われています。多読では、「1. 速く　2. 訳さず英語のまま　3. なるべく辞書を使わず」に読むことが大切です。スピードを計るなど、速く読むよう心がけましょう（たとえば TOEIC® テストの音声スピードはおよそ 1 分間に150 語です）。そして 1 語ずつ訳すのではなく、英語を英語のまま理解するくせをつけるようにします。こうして読み続けるうちに語感がついてきて、だんだんと英語が理解できるようになるのです。まずは、ラダーシリーズの中からあなたのレベルに合った本を選び、少しずつ英文に慣れ親しんでください。たくさんの本を手にとるうちに、英文書がすらすら読めるようになってくるはずです。

《本シリーズの特徴》

- 中学校レベルから中級者レベルまで5段階に分かれています。自分に合ったレベルからスタートしてください。

- クラシックから現代文学、ノンフィクション、ビジネスと幅広いジャンルを扱っています。あなたの興味に合わせてタイトルを選べます。

- 巻末のワードリストで、いつでもどこでも単語の意味を確認できます。レベル1、2では、文中の全ての単語が、レベル3以上は中学校レベル外の単語が掲載されています。

- カバーにヘッドホーンマークのついているタイトルは、オーディオ・サポートがあります。ウェブから購入／ダウンロードし、リスニング教材としても併用できます。

《使用語彙について》

レベル1：中学校で学習する単語約1000語

レベル2：レベル1の単語＋使用頻度の高い単語約300語

レベル3：レベル1の単語＋使用頻度の高い単語約600語

レベル4：レベル1の単語＋使用頻度の高い単語約1000語

レベル5：語彙制限なし

Contents

【本書に出てくる主なSDGs関連語】

aquaculture	水産養殖
awareness barrier	意識の壁
bio toilet	バイオトイレ
biodiversity	生物学的多様性
bioenergy	バイオエネルギー
biosphere	生物圏
carbon cycle	炭素循環
child abuse	児童虐待
chronic hunger	慢性飢餓
climate change refugee	気候変動避難民
conservation	保護, 保管, 保存
Corruption Perceptions Index (CPI)	腐敗認識指数
deforestation	森林伐採
depopulation	人口 (の) 減少, 過疎 (化)
deportation	(外国人の) 国外退去
desertification	砂漠化
digital divide	情報格差
endangered wildlife species	絶滅のおそれのある野生生物種
extinction	絶滅, 死滅
fair trade	フェアトレード
food aid	食糧援助 [支援]
food drive	フードドライブ
food loss	フードロス
food mileage	フードマイレージ
food waste	フードウェイスト
fossil fuel	化石燃料
fundraising	資金 [寄付金] 集め
geothermal	地熱エネルギー
heat wave	熱波, (長期間の) 酷暑

hotspot	ホットスポット
indigenous people	先住民 (族)
ICT (information and communication technology)	情報通信技術
information barrier	情報の壁
information poor	情報弱者
internally displaced person	国内避難民
landfill	埋め立て (地)
LDC (least developed country)	後発開発途上国
microplastics	マイクロプラスチック
mitigation	緩和, 軽減
overfishing	魚の乱獲
overpopulation	人口過剰
Pacific Garbage Patch	太平洋ゴミベルト
persecution	迫害, 虐待
photosynthesis	光合成
physical barrier	物理的な壁
pie chart	円グラフ, 分円図
plastic bit	小さなプラスチック片
plastic waste	プラスチック廃棄物
poverty cycle	貧困の循環
Red List	レッドリスト
refillable product	詰め替え用製品
renewable energy	再生可能エネルギー
sharing ride	ライドシェア
subtitling technology	字幕技術
sudden hunger	急性飢餓
sustainable	支えられる, 持続できる
trafficking	不正 [不法] 取引, 密売
virtual water	バーチャルウォーター, 仮想水

Introduction to SDGs

Goals for a Better Planet

What are SDGs?

SDGs (Sustainable Development Goals) are the goals made by the United Nations (UN) for creating a new type of society. Right now, there are various problems in the world, such as poverty, hunger, the environment, human rights, etc. The earth itself is nearing its limits as the world's population continues to grow incredibly fast. Until now, little has been done to fix these problems.

However, at a UN meeting in 2015, people from around the world decided to create 17 goals and 169 targets to achieve by 2030. They wanted people everywhere to move toward what is known as "sustainable development."

Sustainable development is a way of planning for the future that tries to balance the needs of people, the environment, and the economy. It means that we should not use up or damage the natural resources and ecosystems that we depend on, and that we should make sure that everyone has a fair chance to live a good life. The 17 goals were created to make sure that countries all over the world were developing in a way that was sustainable.

These are the 17 goals:

1. No poverty
2. Zero hunger
3. Good health and well-being
4. Quality education
5. Gender equality
6. Clean water and sanitation
7. Affordable and clean energy
8. Good jobs and economic growth
9. Build the foundation for industry and innovation
10. Reduce inequality
11. Make cities and communities sustainable
12. Responsible consumption and production
13. Climate action
14. Protect life below water
15. Protect life on land

16. Peace, justice, and strong institutions
17. Achieve the goals through partnership

All these goals are connected. For example, by taking action against global warming (Goal 13), problems in the sea and on land can be reduced (Goals 14 and 15). This would also help with problems like poverty and hunger (Goals 1 and 2). If we have quality education (Goal 4), it will help to improve poverty (Goal 1), and make people understand that men and women are equal (Goals 5 and 10). It could also help to create good jobs and economic growth (Goal 8).

The SDG Wedding Cake Model

To understand how SDGs work, let's look at the Wedding Cake Model. The SDG goals are divided into three layers: Economy, Society, and Biosphere.

The biosphere is the bottom layer because it

is the foundation for everything else. It includes the natural systems that support life, such as the climate, water, and the soil. The society layer is in the middle because it depends on the biosphere and affects the economy. It includes the social and cultural parts of human life, such as education, justice, and equality. The economy layer is on top because it is the result of human activity and choices. It includes the production and consumption of goods and services, such as agriculture, industry, and trade.

Right now, the SDG wedding cake is out of balance. The economy layer is too big. This means that the economic activities of humans are harming the biosphere and society. For example, burning oil and gas for energy causes climate change, which affects the weather, crops, and people's health. Cutting down forests for wood destroys the places where animals make their homes. These are some of the problems that the SDGs will help to solve.

To make the SDG wedding cake more balanced, the economy layer needs to be smaller, and it needs to fit within the other layers. This means that the economic activities of humans need to fit inside the limits of the biosphere and the needs of society. For example, using clean energy, such as solar power, can slow down climate change. Planting more trees and

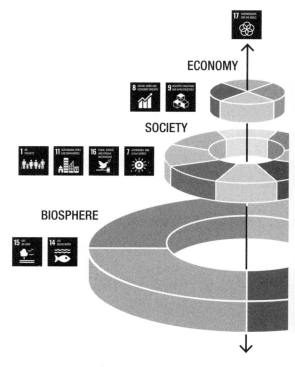

protecting natural areas can save animals and improve air quality. Recycling products can save resources and prevent waste and pollution. These are some of the actions that the SDGs encourage.

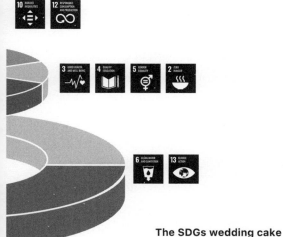

The SDGs wedding cake

Azote for Stockholm Resilience centre, Stockholm University CC BY-ND3.0.

Goal 1 ·····································

No Poverty

···

SDG 1 is the first goal for making the world a better place. We need to end every kind of poverty in every place and for every person. Poverty means that people do not have enough of the things they need to live, such as food, water, health, or education. It causes problems like hunger, sickness, and violence.

One of the targets of SDG 1 is to stop extreme poverty, which means that no one should have to live on less than $2.15 a day. Another is to give people access to services and support, such as money, health care, and education. It will also be important to make sure that all people have the same rights and opportunities to be success-ful in life. For this, they have to be able to own land and tools, use technology, and earn money.

Poverty in Japan and the World

Experts say that in Japan, a person is living in poverty if they make less than ¥100,000 per month. One in six (15.4 percent) people and one in seven (13.5 percent) children in Japan live in poverty.

Poverty is a very serious problem here in Japan, but things are much worse in other countries. It is said that about one in four people in the world do not have enough money for basic things such as food, homes, education, and medicine. Even worse, about 700 million people are living in absolute poverty. They often suffer from terrible hunger and sickness. And they usually have no power or voice to change their situation.

The Poverty Cycle

The poverty cycle is a pattern that causes people to become and then stay poor. It can also continue from one generation to the next. The poverty cycle has many causes and effects, and it is hard to break without help.

One reason for the poverty cycle is a low salary. People who do not get enough money may not have enough food, water, health care, education, or other things they need. They may suffer from hunger, sickness, and lack of knowledge. These problems make it harder for them to do well in their work and earn more money. Such people are likely to have low savings. This means they cannot invest in things that can improve their lives, such as better tools, land, or skills.

Child grows up in poverty

Disadvantage in education and skills

Family in poverty

Poverty Cycle

Low personal income

Struggles to get a job

It is said that in Japan, there are many children who do not get enough food every day. As a result, they are likely to feel hungry at school, and this can make it more difficult to listen to the teacher and study. Their grades may not be as good as those of other students. Without good grades, they may not be able to go to university or get a good job. Being hungry as a child can affect their whole lives, and also the lives of their children.

The poverty cycle has many negative effects on people and the environment. Poor people have lower well-being and happiness. They may also lose hope and confidence. They also may not be able to participate in society and democracy. The poverty cycle can also damage the environment because poor people may use natural resources in unsustainable ways, such as cutting down trees or polluting water.

What Can Be Done?

Some ways that countries, groups, and other

organizations can make poor people's lives better are by giving them things they need every day, such as water, electricity, roads, or trains. It is also good to give them food to stop hunger. But, in the end, we have to help them help themselves. For example, people from Japan can go to other countries to teach people about technology that will make the lives of farmers and workers better, or to train doctors.

We also need to think about ways to use the money that rich people and big companies make to help society, and to make sure that people who are old or poor have  enough money. Small things that people can do are giving money or things to poor people or buying fair trade products. Fair trade means buying things made in poor countries at fair prices that let farmers make enough money. There are different kinds of fair trade chocolate, coffee, bags, and so on, and these things always have the Fairtrade symbol on them.

Goal 2···

Zero Hunger

SDG 2 is to end hunger, to make sure that everyone has enough good food, and to help farmers grow food in a way that does not harm the environment. Hunger can make people sick, weak, and unhappy, and it can stop them from learning, working, and growing.

One target is to give more food to people who do not have enough, especially children, women, and poor people. Another is to make food cheaper and easier to get. It is also important to raise the quality and variety of food so people can get all the nutrients they need. The UN is also trying to help farmers use better tools, machines, land, and skills so they can grow more food and make more money. Finally, efforts are being made to protect the environment from the effects of farming, such as cutting down trees, polluting water, or wasting food.

Hunger in the World

One in nine people in the world suffers from hunger. Although hunger is terrible for everyone, it is especially serious for children. One out of every four children in the world will not be able to fully develop mentally and physically because they are not getting enough healthy food.

Food Waste and Food Loss

Every year, about 1.3 billion tons of food are thrown out or destroyed. That's one-third of all the food that is produced in the world! In Japan, it is said that an average person wastes 42 kilograms of food every year.

When experts talk about this problem, they use two different phrases, "food waste" and "food loss." These two important problems happen at different stages of the food journey. Food waste happens mostly in stores, restaurants, and people's homes. For example, restaurants might throw out food if they don't have enough customers. It can also happen when we buy too much food at the store, and some of it goes bad in our homes.

On the other hand, food loss happens during production and transportation. For instance, if fruit and vegetables get damaged while they are still growing or while being sent to the store, that is food loss. Sometimes, food can also be lost because it does not look nice enough to sell, even if it is still good to eat.

Overpopulation

Overpopulation reduces the amount of land, water, and energy available for growing food. This means that there is less food for more people, and food prices go up. Many people cannot afford to buy enough food for themselves and their families. Overpopulation also makes climate change worse, which affects the weather and the crops. Climate change causes more droughts, floods, and storms, which damage farms and the environment. This leads to lower food production and quality, and more hunger and worse nutrition.

War and Natural Disasters

War and disasters affect millions of people around the world, especially in developing countries. They make it harder for people to grow or buy enough food to stay healthy.

Wars can destroy the farms and food supplies of people who live in conflict areas. This means that they have less food to eat or sell. Wars can also force people to leave their homes and their land. Such people often have to live in camps or shelters, where they depend on food aid to survive. Sometimes, the aid is not enough or is blocked by groups that are fighting.

Disasters can also damage or destroy the

crops and animals of farmers, reducing their food production and income. They can also affect the quality and safety of the food that is available. Furthermore, they can make it difficult or impossible for people to reach the markets or the shops where they can buy food. They can also cause problems with the transportation and distribution of food.

What Can Be Done?

There are sometimes said to be two kinds of hunger: sudden hunger and chronic hunger. Sudden hunger happens when something unexpected makes food hard to get, such as when bad weather damages farmers' crops. The media reports a lot about it, so people can quickly help by giving money and goods. Chronic hunger is not as easy to notice, but it is more severe and lasts longer. To end chronic hunger, we need to improve the facilities and systems that are used for food production. However, rich countries should not just build them or give poor countries what they do not have. They should also teach them how to farm sustainably so they can make their own food in the future.

In Japan, most of the food comes from other countries. People can reduce food waste by cooking and buying only what they need. We can also eat more local food. Another way to help is to do a food drive. This means collecting food for people who do not have enough. People bring extra food from their homes to places like schools or offices and then give it to people or groups that need it. These actions are small, but they can make a difference in Japan and the world.

Goal 3 ·······································

Good Health and Well-Being

SDG 3 is to make sure that people of all ages in all countries can enjoy healthy lives and well-being. This means that everyone should be able to get quality health care, medicines, vaccines, and prevention services.

Some of the targets for SDG 3 are to lower the number of women who die while having babies, to make children healthier, to find cures for diseases like AIDS and malaria, to help people with mental health problems, to stop people from using large amounts of alcohol or drugs, and to promote road safety and healthy lifestyles. Reaching these targets would save millions of lives and improve the quality of life for many more.

Vaccines

Vaccine programs are an important part of SDG 3. It is said that vaccinations for children prevent four million deaths around the world every year. Not only can they help prevent people from getting various diseases, but they can also save money and resources for health care. People who are vaccinated may not need to spend money on medicines or hospital visits. They can also avoid losing income or education due to illness. This can improve their living standards and well-being.

Sadly, though, one out of every five children does not have a chance to receive vaccines. In addition, many people were afraid to get vaccines against the Coronavirus during the pandemic. There is still much work to be done to achieve the United Nations vaccine goals.

Lifestyle Diseases

Another serious problem that the United Nations is working on is lifestyle diseases. These are caused by the way we live. Things like smoking, drinking too much, not exercising, being overweight, and having stress can cause problems like cancer, heart disease, and diabetes.

In the past, these problems were mostly in developed countries, but they are becoming more and more common in developing ones as well. Some scientists believe that 44.4 percent of all cancers around the world could be prevented by things like eating healthier food and stopping smoking. The UN is working to educate people about healthy lifestyle choices and is encouraging governments to make policies that will make people healthier.

What Can Be Done?

The United Nations is working to make sure everyone can get health care that is not too expensive. This is called Universal Health Coverage (UHC). UHC means that everyone can get health services like check-ups, medicines, vaccines, and operations. To make this happen, countries are helping each other by providing things like mosquito nets to stop diseases, cheap and effective medicines, more doctors and nurses, and better hospitals.

One thing we can do is to give money to groups that help with health care in other countries. There are many groups on the internet, but some of them may not be honest, so we should check them carefully before giving them money. If we want to work in health care or help people in need in the future, we can look at Doctors Without Borders, a group that helps people who need medical care because of war, disasters, or poverty. Staff from Doctors without Borders travel to places all over the world where help is urgently needed.

Goal 4 ·····································

Quality Education

SDG 4 is to make sure that everyone has the chance to get a good education. Everyone should be able to get an education and also to continue learning for their whole life.

One target is to make sure that all girls and boys can go to school for free. Another is to help people, especially young adults, learn the skills they need for work and life. Quality education means schools should be safe and welcoming for everyone. To do this, teachers need a lot of training. One other target is to increase the number of people who can read and do basic math.

Literacy

According to UNESCO, literacy is "the ability to read and write simple sentences necessary for daily life." As of 2022, there were believed to be about 773 million people worldwide who could not read or write. Many of those have grown up without education for various reasons, including poverty, war, disrespect for women, and not having schools near their homes. In particular, the number of children between the ages of 6 and 14 who are unable to go to school in developing countries is estimated to be as high as 121 million. The main reason for this is poverty, with children working to make money for their families to live instead of going to school. In the case of girls, there is the belief that education is not necessary in order to get married early and focus on housework and childcare. Of course, child labor is not allowed in Japan, but it is important to know that there are many children in the world who have to work in the fields, walk a long way to get water, or pick up garbage to earn money every day instead of receiving an education.

The Deep Connection between Poverty and Illiteracy

As can be seen from the below illustration, low literacy often leads to low productivity because a person cannot find a good job. As a result, the person often has a low income. This leads to low investment in education because the person cannot spend money on school for their

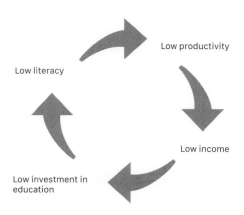

children. This means that the person's children cannot learn to read and write. It can easily become an endless loop.

Not being able to read, write, and do simple math makes it difficult to get skills for jobs. Also, because people cannot read contracts and other documents, they can easily be tricked into working in poor conditions for low pay. Also, not being able to read signs in dangerous places or not being able to read medication labels can put people's lives in danger. To break this cycle, it will be necessary to improve the educational environment by building schools and increasing the number of teachers.

Truancy in Japan

According to a survey in 2020, there were 132,777 junior high school students who were not going to school in Japan. However, if we include students who spend time outside the classroom, such as in the nurse's room or library, and those who arrive late or leave early, the actual number is believed to be more than three times higher. The early teenage years are a tough time for everyone, when many changes are happening in a person's mind and body. Young people may feel that going to school is boring or a nuisance, but if they can find something fun to do during their junior high school life, they may feel more motivated to go there. These days, educational support centers, free schools, tutoring schools, and online schools allow students to learn things they are interested in at their own pace.

What Can Be Done?

We can help people in other countries by donating money to NGOs and organizations working on educational problems. However, it is often better to specify how we want the money to be used. For example, if we want it to go toward school construction or teacher training, it is better to donate to an organization focused on that area. Some organizations also send used school bags with supplies like notebooks and pencils to countries in need. You can find various organizations accepting donations on the internet.

Goal 5 ·····································

Gender Equality

SDG 5 is to make sure that men and women have the same chances in all aspects of life. One important target is ending discrimination and violence based on gender. Another goal is to recognize and value unpaid work, like taking care of children and housework, which are often done by women.

One target is to give women the chance to express their opinions and take part in politics and lawmaking. Another is ending child marriage.

Gender equality means creating a fair society in which everyone, no matter what sex they are, is treated equally and with respect. It is about breaking down barriers and making a world where men and women can work together to build a better future.

Domestic Violence

Domestic violence is a big problem, especially for women. It includes hurting one's partner physically or emotionally. It is said that one in three women around the world experience domestic or sexual violence in their lifetime. The UN is trying to get countries to make new laws that will stop violence against women and also to promote educational programs that will teach people why domestic and sexual violence are wrong.

Unpaid Work

Unpaid work is a problem because many people do important jobs, such as cooking and cleaning, without getting paid for them. Most of the time, it is women who do these things. According to UN Women, this unpaid work is worth a lot of money, between 10 and 39 percent of a country's total income.

A survey in Japan from 2018 found that the value of women's housework for a year was

¥1,935,000. Women also spend about 2.5 times more time than men doing unpaid work like cleaning. Because they spend so much time on unpaid work, women often earn less than men in paid jobs, creating a gap between them. In many places, there is a tradition that women do housework while men work outside to support the family. Changing this way of thinking is necessary to reduce gender inequality and unpaid work.

Child Marriage

Child marriage is when children who are younger than 18 get married. Every year, 12 million girls who are younger than 18 are forced to get married. Child marriage happens mostly in poor places, like Africa and India, where parents or relatives sell girls to men for money. Girls who are married too young lose their freedom and the chance to get an education. They can also die because of having babies when they are not ready. Child marriage will not stop until we fix problems like poverty, old customs, weak laws, and people who do not care.

Political Equality

Political equality means that everyone has an equal say in decisions. It is necessary to have fair societies. Unfortunately, women often do not have the same political rights as men. Globally, women make up only around 24 percent of people in government. In countries like Sweden, where more effort has been made regarding SDG 5, women's participation in political decision-making has increased greatly.

Voting rights are also very important. In some places, women have not been allowed to vote for religious or cultural reasons. However, being able to choose the leaders of a country is a basic right for everyone, so SDG 5 is trying to make sure that every adult in the world is able to vote.

What Can Be Done?

Gender inequality is an important issue that comes from traditions in our society that have been around for hundreds or even thousands of years. It is so deeply rooted that many people do not even think about it, as in the case of unpaid work. But it is important to make things equal between men and women because it can help reduce poverty and improve education.

The first step is to understand what the problems are. If there are things the government, society, or companies are doing that we can be a part of, we should join in. In our daily lives, doing small things like sharing work at home can also make a difference.

Some people think the way we treat young children is very important. Maybe we should not buy blue clothes for boys and pink for girls. And the toys we buy may be important too. Why not buy chemistry sets for our daughters or toy cooking stoves for our sons?

Also, it is important to understand that every person is different, and we should not think that men or women have to act in a certain way. We should always try to treat everyone fairly and without bias.

Goal 6·····································

Clean Water and Sanitation

SDG 6 is to make sure that everyone has access to clean water and proper sanitation. This goal is important for people's health and for preventing diseases caused by unsafe water. The main target is making sure that everyone can get clean, safe drinking water that is not too far away from their homes. Another is improving sanitation facilities around the world. Many people still do not have basic toilets and proper waste disposal, leading to health risks. Additionally, the goal encourages the protection and restoration of water-related ecosystems. Preserving water sources like rivers and lakes will help everyone to have clean drinking water.

The Earth's Water

About 97 percent of the earth's surface is salt water, and only 3 percent is fresh water. Of that 3 percent, 70 percent is in the form of glaciers, 29 percent is groundwater, and the remaining

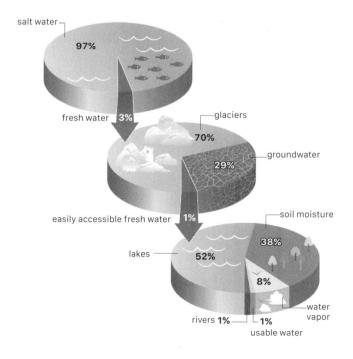

1 percent is usable water. In reality, however, of this 1 percent, 46 percent is water vapor and soil moisture, and 53 percent is lakes and rivers of poor quality, so only 1 percent of that is usable. The earth's usable water supply is like one spoonful (20 milliliters) of water in a bathtub (200 liters). The world's water problems are becoming serious due to climate change, population growth, and the increasing need to use water for growing food and for business.

Drinking Water

There are only 15 countries in the world where you can drink tap water directly from the tap, and there are many countries that do not even have tap water. There are also countries where there is not enough water. It is believed that about 2.2 billion people in the world cannot get safe drinking water. In some developing countries, water is taken from rivers and lakes filled with pollution and dead animals and used as drinking water. Even if this water is boiled, it is not safe, especially for children. Some countries are developing systems to make seawater usable through the use of technology.

Water and Population Growth

As the number of people increases, so does the amount of water used for daily life and industrial purposes, such as manufacturing. In addition, global warming and water and soil pollution are making the world's water shortages worse. As global warming increases, typhoons, floods, and droughts are more likely to happen. Floods may sound like they would temporarily make water shortages better, but they can cause damage to infrastructure that is needed for cleaning and transporting water.

Water and soil contamination are also serious problems. If sewage infrastructure is not good, excrement and household waste will flow directly into rivers and ponds. Polluted water containing chemicals from factories is also a big problem.

Water in Developing Countries

In developing countries, there are people who have to go to get the water they need every day. This job is usually given to women and children, and they walk an average of about 6 kilometers round trip every day to get water. Even if they carry 20 liters of water at a time, that is only enough for one person to use for a day, so they must make several trips to get enough for their families.

If children did not have to carry water, they could go to school during this time, and women could work to get money. NGOs in various countries are working to put in wells and water tanks closer to homes to help families have safe water.

Toilets

About 4.2 billion people, mainly in developing countries, do not have access to safe and clean toilets. In fact, about one in three people relieve themselves in a place other than the so-called toilet. For example, they may dig a hole in the ground outdoors and cover it with soil when they are done or defecate in a pond or river. This leads to contamination of drinking water and causes infectious diseases, such as dysentery. Between 800 and 1,000 babies die every day from diseases caused by water that is not clean.

In areas where water and toilet problems exist, efforts are being made to improve water and sewage infrastructure and to develop and spread bio toilets that use microorganisms to dispose of waste without the use of water.

Virtual Water

Virtual water is an idea that helps us understand the hidden water used in making the things we use every day. It is not the water we drink or see. It is the water needed to produce the food we eat, the clothes we wear, and even the products we use.

For example, a large amount of water is required to produce each ingredient in a hamburger, such as wheat, lettuce, and beef. In some places, it is thought that about 2,400 liters of water are used to produce one hamburger. If we assume that all of the ingredients for a hamburger are imported, the virtual water consumption would be 2,400 liters.

What Can Be Done?

International cooperation is very important to improve water supply and sewage systems, install wells, and develop technology to produce fresh water from seawater. We must not only build facilities, but also teach local people about the technology, work with them to develop and think of solutions that suit their local needs, and teach children hygiene practices as part of their education.

One of the most important things individuals can do is learn about ways to save water. If you leave the water running when you wash your face, you are wasting about 12 liters of water per minute. If you leave the water running in the shower for 3 minutes, about 36 liters of water will be used. Saving water is not only good for the environment, but it saves money, too. For example, if you use a cup of water when brushing your teeth, you can save about 5 liters of water, and for a family of three, you can save about ¥220 a month by brushing your teeth this way. Also, when washing dishes, pans, and other greasy items, if you first wipe off the grease with paper towels, you will use less water and detergent, and you will also protect the entire planet from water pollution by not pouring oil into the sewage system.

Goal 7 ·····································

Affordable and Clean Energy

SDG 7 is to have affordable, reliable, sustainable, and modern energy for all. It is important because we need so much energy in our daily lives and energy affects our health, education, and economic opportunities.

One of the targets is to make sure that everyone can use affordable and clean energy. This means making sure everyone can use energy that does not harm the environment and is reasonably priced. Another target is to increase the use of renewable energy. We need to use more sources like the sun and wind, which are better for the planet.

Cooking Fuel

The world's population is about 8 billion. More than 2.5 billion people burn wood or charcoal to cook. In other words, about one-third of the world's population still does not have electricity or gas, so they cook with dangerous and inefficient fuels. Indoor use of wood or charcoal can cause carbon monoxide poisoning if the air cannot move in and out of a building easily. Also, smoke and soot contain many harmful substances that can make people sick.

Fossil Fuels and Global Warming

Global warming is caused by fossil fuel use and also by deforestation. Fossil fuels, such as oil and charcoal, make up about 90 percent of the world's energy sources, but the gases produced by burning them are terrible for the environment. They go up into the atmosphere and trap heat. As a result, the global average temperature is likely to rise 2.8 °C by the end of the 21st century, and sea levels will rise by between 30 cm and 1 m. Even a small increase in temperature will cause flooding in areas near the sea, cause more forest fires, and make it harder to grow food.

Renewable Energy

Renewable energy comes from energy sources that can be used repeatedly, such as solar and wind energy. Other types include hydroelectric, geothermal, bioenergy, and wave power. Japan ranked eighth (18 percent) in the percentage of renewable energy use in the nine leading countries in fiscal year 2019, compared with Canada (66 percent), which ranked first. This shows that Japan still relies heavily on fossil fuels.

Renewable energies are wonderful, but there is a problem with them. The amount of power they can produce depends on the season, the weather, and even the time of day. For example, in northern countries, it is much easier to get solar energy in the summer than in the winter, and clouds can cover the sun. And of course, there is no sun at night. To make solar and other types of renewable energy, we need to find better ways to store it. For example, scientists are working to create better batteries that are smaller and can hold more energy for a longer time.

The Paris Agreement

In 2015 at COP21, countries from around the world signed The Paris Agreement. Five years earlier, at COP16, a target was set to limit the global average temperature increase to within 2 °C. At COP21, a new, lower goal of 1.5 °C was set.

A 2 °C increase in average temperature will raise sea levels by an average of about 10 cm by 2100. This would increase the number of people whose lives will be affected by water shortages by 50 percent. The amount of food we can get from crops would go down by about 7 percent, and we would lose 99 percent of the coral reefs around the world. For the 1.5 °C target, we must reduce carbon dioxide emissions in 2030 to 45 percent lower than the levels in 2010, and further reduce carbon dioxide emissions to zero by 2050.

According to one report, the global average temperature for the period from 1850 to 2020 has already increased by 1.09 °C. If this continues, the temperature is expected to rise by 2.8 °C by the end of this century, so SDG 7 is very important.

What Can Be Done?

Developed countries must become leaders in slowing global warming by reducing the use of fossil fuels, developing renewable energy, and providing infrastructure support, such as electricity and gas, to developing countries.

In Japan, we can take small actions, such as saving electricity, taking trains and buses instead of cars, and using recycled products to reduce the use of fossil fuels.

In addition, there may be more disasters,

such as typhoons and floods, in the future, so it is a good idea to check where to evacuate and how to contact your family.

Goal 8 ······································

Good Jobs and Economic Growth

SDG 8 is to create decent work and economic growth for everyone. All people should be able to find good jobs and be treated fairly when they are working. Jobs are not just important for individual people. They also help to build strong communities.

One target of SDG 8 is that everyone who wants a job can find one that gives them a good salary and good working conditions. Another target focuses on reducing the number of young people who are not in education, employment, or training. They need skills and opportunities so they can start their careers and make the economy stronger. Another target is to create safe working environments for all workers. This includes protecting workers' rights and making sure they are safe on the job.

Unemployment

There are about 220 million people around the world who do not have jobs. This not only makes it difficult for them to buy food, stay healthy, and live in a safe, comfortable home, but it can be very stressful and lead to mental health problems as well.

It is agreed that one of the best ways to reduce unemployment is through education and training, so many of the targets of SDG 8 are to make sure that people can read and write and have the skills they need to get good jobs. In particular, there is a focus on helping young adults who need more training to get jobs.

Underemployment

Unemployment is not the only job-related problem that people have. There are also millions more people in the world who are underemployed. That means that they have a job, but they do not get enough salary to support themselves and their families. Today, many companies are changing the way they do business, and there are fewer full-time jobs available. Many companies want to hire temporary workers and freelancers. These are people who do not work for the company. Instead, they are hired to do work at the company for a short time, or to work on special projects, such as a web designer who is hired to make a website for a company. SDG 8 has targets that encourage countries to create policies that support not only job creation but also the quality of jobs. This includes making sure that people have opportunities for full-time work that uses their skills effectively.

Child Labor

Around the world, about 160 million children between the ages of 5 and 17 have to work in jobs. That is about 1 in every 10 children. About half of them (79 million) have jobs that are dangerous. Poor families sometimes send their children to work outside the home to increase their income, but children's pay is so low that even if they work from morning to night, they earn only a small amount of money. Child labor is considered to be forced labor because the child would never choose to work, and it is against the law. Reducing it is an important SDG target.

What Can Be Done?

One thing everyone can do is to support local businesses by buying products and services from them. This helps businesses grow and creates more jobs in the community. We can also make choices that promote fair work. When shopping, we can look for products with labels that show they were made under good working conditions. And if we hear about a company that is not treating its workers well, we can stop buying its products. Additionally, learning new skills or improving existing ones can help us find jobs. Finally, we can talk to others about the importance of decent work and economic growth, encouraging a collective effort to create positive changes. Even small actions, like sharing information on social media, can help build a world where all adults can get good jobs.

Goal 9 ··

Build the Foundation for Industry and Innovation

··

SDG 9 is to make industries and infrastructure better by building strong and sustainable economic growth for everyone. It encourages countries to spend money on innovation, technology, and infrastructure to create job opportunities and improve people's lives.

One target is to make good, strong, and lasting infrastructure, such as buildings and roads that help the economy. Another is to help small businesses and make sure they have enough money. Also, we need to use more science and better technology to come up with new ideas and solutions.

Infrastructure in Developing Countries

Many of the railroads and highways in places like Africa, South America, and Asia were constructed when the countries were colonies of European nations. Especially in Africa, after the countries became independent, the infra-structure was not maintained well. As a result, much of it is in poor condition. It is said that just 9 percent of roads in sub-Saharan African countries are paved. In addition, the railroads are getting older, and it is becoming difficult to move goods around. In many countries, there are few ports that can accept large cargo ships, and long waiting times have become a serious problem. All of this is hurting developing countries' growth. Therefore, it is important to improve the railroads, roads, and ports.

The Need for Research

LDC stands for least developed country. These are nations that are particularly underde-veloped, even among developing countries.

SDG 9 includes targets to support technology development, research, and innovation, but it is difficult for high-tech industries to grow in LDCs. One reason is that there is not enough money for research and development.

Also, the number of researchers per million people in developed countries is 3,739, and the global average number of researchers is said to be 1,098 per million people. However, the number is only 63 per million in the least developed countries. Not only money but basic education for all people is needed so that more people have the chance to become researchers. Higher-level education is also needed so that they can make advances that help reduce poverty.

The Digital Divide

In developed countries in 2021, 90 percent of people had access to the internet. However, this number was just 57 percent in developing countries, and it was just 27 percent in LDCs. People who do not have access to ICT (information and communication technology) are referred to as the "information poor." The huge number of the information poor in developing countries is serious because it affects everything from education to health care to the economy. In order to reduce the information gap, national and local governments need to support the use of ICT, provide free devices, and develop human resources in the IT industry.

Green Infrastructure

Green infrastructure is about creating and using natural solutions to make our cities, homes, and transportation systems better. It helps with SDG 9 by making our buildings and roads stronger and friendlier to the environment. For example, instead of just using concrete and steel, green infrastructure includes things like parks, trees, and plants.

One way green infrastructure is linked to SDG 9 is by making our cities more resilient. This means they can better handle problems like floods or extreme weather. When we have green spaces and trees, they can absorb water and give us shade, making our cities safer and more pleasant. Green infrastructure also supports using clean and renewable energy sources, like solar or wind power. This helps us move away from using too much energy that can harm the environment.

What Can Be Done?

Even though Japan is a developed country, it has not been as quick as others to make use of ICT technology. This was clear during the COVID-19 pandemic when schools closed and companies started letting their staff work from home. Using more technology in government and health care makes life better, but it is taking a long time for these changes to happen.

So, what can we do to help? Donating money for better infrastructure in developing countries is a good idea, but we need to be careful that it is used the right way. It is better to send money through trusted organizations. Also, volunteering with a Japanese group that supports local activities is helpful. Learning IT and ICT skills is important for the future. It helps us think in logical and creative ways to solve problems. Developing these skills can show us how to make society and companies better more quickly.

Goal 10 ·····································

Reduce Inequality

···

SDG 10 is about making the world more equal. We need to make sure that everyone, no matter where they come from or who they are, has the same chances in life. The main goal is to decrease the gap between rich and poor. This is important because when some people have a lot and others have very little, it can create problems like poverty and social tension.

One target is to increase the income growth of the poorest people. By helping those with less money, we can make sure they have a better life. Another target is to make sure everyone has the same rights. Discrimination can make life harder for some people, so the goal is to treat everyone fairly.

The Wealth Gap

If you add up all the wealth owned by the 26 richest people in the world, it would be the same as the amount of wealth owned by the poorest 50 percent of the world's population. That means that just 26 people have the same amount of wealth as about 4 billion people! Things like taxes, welfare, and public works projects can help to redistribute the wealth so that everyone is closer together. For example, in Japan's health insurance system, younger people who are healthy and have high incomes pay higher amounts of money, while elderly people with low incomes pay less to use hospitals. On the other hand, there is currently no global mechanism for the redistribution of wealth among nations.

Immigration

The pie chart shows which regions of the world people were migrating to in the year 2020. The largest number of migrants went to Europe,

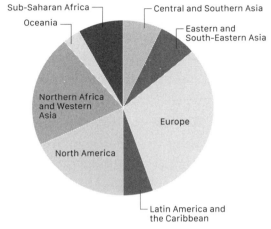

UN DESA, Population Division (2020b).
International Migrant Stock 2020.

with 87 million, followed by North America, with 59 million, and North Africa and West Asia, with 50 million. The country that received the most immigrants was the United States, which received 51 million. That is 18 percent of the world's total. Other countries with large numbers of immigrants included Germany (16 million), Saudi Arabia (13 million), and Russia (12 million). In 2020, the total number of international migrants worldwide was 281 million.

The main reasons that so many people migrate to other countries are poverty and unemployment. Sometimes, things are so bad in people's home countries that they try to enter another country illegally. However, illegal immigrants may not be able to find employment and escape poverty. Often, they cannot get social security and medical care, and they may be forced to work for unfair salaries. Countries that accept immigrants have introduced policies, such as increased security and deportation, to keep illegal immigrants out, while at the same time protecting the rights of regular immigrants and giving them welfare. In order to prevent further migration, developed countries will need to provide assistance to developing countries to create an environment in which people can work and live comfortably.

The Income Gap between Men and Women

In a study of the income gap between men and women, Japan ranked third worst among the 42 countries and areas, along with South Korea and Israel. The graph of the wage gap between men and women in the seven major countries shows the difference between men's wages and women's wages. The larger the percentage is, the wider the gap. Japan's wage gap between men and women is 22.5 percent, whereas the average for OECD member countries is 11.6 percent.

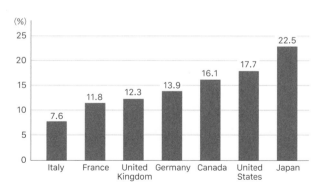

OECD. Gender Gap of Leading Nations (2020)

The causes of the wage gap include the customs and traditions that affect the roles of men and women in society, and the lack of systems and services for childcare and nursing care.

Refugees

Refugees are people who have escaped across countries' borders to other nations for various reasons, including discrimination, war, political persecution, economic problems, and natural disasters. People who have to leave their homes for similar reasons but do not cross borders are called internally displaced persons. In 2021, there were 27.1 million refugees and 53.2 million internally displaced persons.

The places with the most refugees are developing countries. Unfortunately, they often do not have enough money to take care of refugees. Many have to live in refugee camps, and the number of refugees is so large that there is never enough money and food to take care of them. In addition, lack of clean water, good food, medical care, and hygiene can cost lives. Developed countries give money to refugee camps, and Japan gave about 13.38 billion yen to the UN to help refugees in 2019.

Fair Trade

Things become products and reach customers through the hands of various people. As shown in the illustration, chocolate begins with farmers who grow cacao beans. Then there are processors and manufacturers who make the

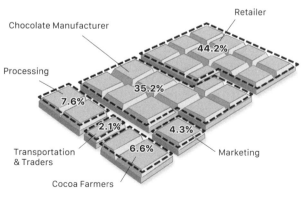

Cocoa Barometer 2015

ingredients into chocolate. Finally, the products are bought by companies that sell them in stores.

Cacao beans are mainly grown in developing countries, most of which are in Africa and South America. Cacao farmers receive only 6.6 percent of the price of chocolate. This is because companies from developed countries buy the ingredients cheaply and then make a lot of money from turning them into chocolate and selling them at a high price. The farmers will always be poor if cacao beans are traded at low prices.

Fair trade is an effort to improve this unfair system. The World Fair Trade Organization (WFTO) and other groups have created fair trade rules to try to stop things like forced labor, child labor, discrimination, and environmental damage in the production process.

Equality

One might think that in order to stop inequality, everyone must be "equal." But actually, it

equality   equity

is more important that things are "fair." The illustration is a good example of the difference. A tall adult, a child, and a person in a wheelchair are watching a soccer game. But there is a high wall in front of them. In the picture on the left, the three people are treated equally and given a box of the same height without thinking about their situation. Thanks to the boxes, the tall adult and the child in the middle can watch the game, but the person in the wheelchair cannot see because she cannot get on the box. The picture on the right shows how the boxes can be moved to match the situation of each of the three people. The boxes can be made into a ramp so that wheelchairs can roll on them. Now, everyone can watch the game fairly. This fairness is the key to stopping inequality. "Eliminating inequality" means respecting the diversity of people's backgrounds and helping them to participate together in society.

What Can Be Done?

In Japan, laws against discrimination and hate speech were created in 2016. However, no matter how many treaties and laws are made, they will not easily lead to the elimination of discrimination, prejudice, and inequality by themselves.

"He's Black, but he's a terrible basketball player." "He's a boy, but he's a good cook." "You should stay away from people who don't wear masks." Have you ever said such things without thinking about the person's background and whether there is any evidence for these things? Words not only hurt people's feelings, but they can also have big effects in the world. They can change the way our children think and act, and they can stop people from giving jobs to minorities or marrying people from other cultures. To avoid racism and discrimination, it is important to do research and find out facts rather than just believing things that our friends tell us or that we learn on social media.

Goal 11 ···································

Make Cities and Communities Sustainable

SDG 11 is to make cities and other communities safe, comfortable, and sustainable. Everyone should have a home and be able to use transportation and enjoy green spaces. One target is to provide housing that is not too expensive for everyone. This goal also says that the homes should be safe and have all the things that people need to live comfortably, such as toilets and things to cook with.

Another target is to improve urban transportation, making it safer and more accessible. This includes better public transportation systems and infrastructure for walking and cycling. There is also a goal to reduce traffic accidents and to make it easier for people to move around their cities.

Additionally, SDG 11 talks about the natural environment in cities. This involves creating more parks and green areas, as well as protecting cultural and historical sites.

Depopulation and Overpopulation

Today, 55 percent of the world's population lives in urban areas. When people live together in large cities, the economy grows faster and life is more convenient. It is much easier to find jobs and get important services, like health care. However, when a lot of people move from the country to cities, it can also cause problems.

Many people are moving from the country to cities to find jobs with higher salaries. However, cities can easily become overcrowded, and there can be serious problems with things like air pollution. As the demand for cars increases, the amount of exhaust gas emissions rises. As industry becomes more active, the number of factories also increases, and these put out large amounts of smoke containing dangerous chemicals that pollute the air.

Some people come to urban areas in search of work but find that they are very poor because they cannot find a job that pays enough. Slums are neighborhoods in urban areas where poor people live. They are often extremely dangerous, the water is not safe to drink, and the living conditions are dirty.

The main cause of depopulation is young people moving to cities. As a result, most people living in depopulated areas are elderly. When rural areas do not have enough people, it is difficult to support public transportation systems and service becomes less convenient. In some cases, the systems stop operating completely. This makes it inconvenient for the elderly to live their daily lives, including shopping and going to the hospital.

People with Disabilities

In order to create a community where everyone can live comfortably, we must create cities that are convenient for people with disabilities. People with disabilities face difficulties in society like physical barriers that make it difficult to move around, information barriers that prevent them from finding out important things, and awareness barriers caused by people not caring or discrimination.

SDG 11 can help with physical barriers by making sure cities have things like ramps and elevators so people with disabilities can move around easily. The goal also helps make sure that people with disabilities have equal opportunities. This means that everyone should have the same chances for jobs, education, etc. SDG 11 also encourages sharing important information in a way that everyone can understand. For example, subtitling technology is helping people who cannot hear well to get news and entertainment on TV. Lastly, SDG 11 promotes understanding and kindness. When people care about each other and do not discriminate, it is easier for everyone, including those with disabilities, to be part of the community.

New Types of Cities

In many cities, large stores and shopping centers are being built in the suburbs, causing the central areas to decline. Many people own cars and live in the suburbs, but as the population ages, those who do not use cars find that their daily lives have become inconvenient. However, there are some ideas for solving this problem.

A compact city is an attempt to reduce the use of cars and make life easier for seniors by building a community that has all the things necessary for daily life, such as housing, health care, shops, and businesses, within a small area. It is expected that compact cities will make it possible to create a sustainable society by improving the convenience of urban areas, reducing the amount of infrastructure, and protecting the environment.

A smart city is one that tries to make people's lives better using ICT technologies, such as AI and big data, to improve convenience and comfort for residents, while taking the environment into consideration. Woven City is the name of a city developed by Toyota Motor Corporation in Susono, Shizuoka Prefecture, on a large site the size of 15 Tokyo Domes. It is a smart city where new technologies, such as self-driving cars, robots, AI, and smart homes (homes where everything can be operated by smartphone apps or voice) are used.

What Can Be Done?

At the country level, governments can do a few important things. First, they should make sure that there are rules about building houses that are safe and not too expensive. This means having laws that stop houses from costing too much and making sure they are built in a way that they will not fall apart.

Governments can also improve public transportation, like buses and trains, so it is easy for everyone to move around cities. It is important to have good roads and sidewalks for walking or cycling too. These changes can make cities safer and more comfortable for everyone.

In our everyday lives, people can also do small things, like using public transportation or sharing rides to reduce traffic. Also, we should be careful about not wasting water and electricity at home. Planting trees or taking care of green spaces in our neighborhoods can make our surroundings healthier and more pleasant.

Goal 12 ································

Responsible Consumption and Production

SDG 12 is about responsible consumption and production. This means using resources wisely and creating goods in ways that do not harm the environment. One target is to use fewer natural resources by reducing waste and doing more recycling.

Another target is to make sure people everywhere understand the importance of living sustainably. This includes teaching them about recycling, reusing, and choosing products that are better for the environment. By doing this, we can create a world where everyone has enough, and the earth stays healthy.

Reducing food waste is also a goal. This means not throwing away food that can still be eaten. By thinking about what we buy and using what we have, we can make sure fewer people go hungry.

Dealing with Waste

It is best to create as little waste as possible, but when there is waste, it is important to make an effort to use it up by thinking, "Is this still usable?" or "Can it be used in place of something else?" before throwing it away.

Here are some things that can be done with garbage:

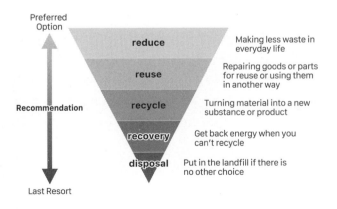

The five ways of dealing with waste

Reduce—A way to create less garbage. You can do this by buying only what you need, using eco-friendly bags, etc.

Reuse—This can be done by using things over and over again, repairing broken items, and buying refillable products so that containers can be used again.

Recycle—This is the process of turning separated garbage back into resources and then reusing them as something new. For example, newspapers can be turned into toilet paper.

Recover—A recycling method in which nonrecyclable waste is burned but part of the heat energy is recovered and used. An example is a heated swimming pool that uses the heat from burned waste.

Disposal—If there is no other choice, then garbage must be put properly into a landfill rather than being thrown out somewhere in a city or in nature.

Fast Fashion

In fast fashion, new clothing styles arrive frequently in stores and are sold at low prices. Brands such as UNIQLO and GU are typical examples. To make the clothes cheaply, however, very large quantities of each type of clothing have to be made. People buy a lot of new clothes because they are cheap and nice looking, but they often throw them away after a short time because buying a lot of low-priced items makes it difficult to develop a love for each one. It is said that an average Japanese person buys about 18 items of clothing per year, gets rid of 12 items, and has about 25 that are not worn. Also, most old clothes in Japan go into the garbage rather than being donated or recycled.

Sadly, in order to make large amounts of cheap clothing, some companies make people work long hours for low pay and do things that damage the environment. It is nice to have cheap clothes, but it is also important to think about how the clothes were created, to buy only what is necessary, and to try to make them last as long as possible.

Food Mileage

Food mileage is the distance it takes for food to reach the consumer from the place of production. Food delivered from far-away places has high food mileage. This is because a lot of energy is used for transportation and storing the food. This means that the related carbon dioxide and other emissions are high, which is bad for the environment.

Japan produces little food for itself and is dependent on imports from other countries. As a result, food eaten in Japan often has high food mileage. This is why the concept of local production for local consumption, which can reduce food mileage, is becoming more popular. If you buy vegetables and fruit grown by local producers and locally processed products at farmers' markets and supermarkets in your area, you can get fresh and safe ingredients with low transportation costs. Producers can also get more money from direct sales, and less food gets wasted when it is not sent to far-away places. Furthermore, the use of locally grown food in school lunches and local restaurants encourages increased food production.

What Can Be Done?

Governments can make laws that promote careful use of resources and lessen waste. They can also teach people about the importance of choosing products wisely. People should buy only what they need and try to use things for a long time. Recycling is very important, so separating trash for recycling is good. Food waste is a big problem, so it is important not to throw away food that is still good to eat. Also, choosing products that are friendly to the environment is a big help.

Goal 13 ·······························

Climate Action

·······································

SDG 13 is about climate action, which means actions that stop the world from getting too hot. The earth's temperature is rising because of people doing things like burning too much coal and oil. This causes problems like floods, droughts, and bad weather.

One important target is to produce more clean energy. This means using things like wind and solar power to make electricity instead of burning oil, gas, and other things that make pollution. Another target is to teach people about climate change so they can understand why it is a problem and how to help. We also need to make sure that our cities are pre-pared for natural disasters by constructing stronger buildings and having better plans for emergencies. Reducing pollution is a big goal, too. We need to use less plastic and find better ways to use and recycle things.

Climate Risk

In 2020, Japan was ranked as having the fourth-highest risk from climate change among 180 countries in the world. The main reason for Japan's ranking is flood damage, which is affected by typhoons and extremely heavy rains from summer to autumn. Among the countries with the highest risks, Mozambique is number 1, Zimbabwe is number 2, and the Bahamas is number 3, followed by Japan at number 4, then Malawi, Afghanistan, India, South Sudan, Nigeria, and Bolivia, in that order.

Japan is the only developed country near the top of the rankings. And even though the number of deaths from natural disasters in Japan was only 290, the country's economic loss was about $29 billion, second only to India's $69 billion. In general, developing countries are more affected by natural disasters, but even developed countries like Japan are having more problems because of weather conditions that become more extreme every year.

Global Warming and Human Health

Global warming can affect people's health in many ways. As the earth gets warmer, extreme weather events, like heat waves, become more common. Heat waves can lead to heat-related illnesses, especially among old people and young children. It is said that half of the world's population faced heat waves during the summer of 2023.

Additionally, rising temperatures lead to the spread of diseases carried by mosquitoes, such as malaria. As disease-carrying insects expand their habitats, more people are at risk. For example, the WHO estimates that climate change is likely to cause an additional 250,000 deaths per year from poor food, malaria, diarrhea, and heat stress between 2030 and 2050.

Climate Change Refugees

People who have to leave their homes because of climate change and things like floods or droughts are called climate change refugees. In 2020, there were about 110 million such people in the world.

Extinction

One of the reasons that many plant and animal species are close to extinction is temperature rise and climate change, which affect these species' habitats. Floods and heavy rains caused by climate change can change the land itself, causing plants and animals to lose their habitats.

In 2021, the Red List of endangered wildlife species had about 40,084 plants and animals on it, up from about 11,000 in 2000. That is an increase of 400 percent in just 20 years. There are 5,775 threatened species on the Red List due to climate change. It is clear that habitat change, drought, storms, floods, and extreme temperatures have done great harm to wildlife over the past 20 years.

Mitigation and Adaptation

There are two things we can do about climate change. The first is called "mitigation." It means reducing emissions of carbon dioxide and other greenhouse gases to slow or stop the warming of the earth. Examples of mitigation include saving electricity, conserving energy, using renewable energy, and increasing forests.

The second is called "adaptation." As temperatures continue to rise, we need to take action to reduce its effects. Humans will need to develop crops that can grow even in high temperatures, construct stronger buildings in areas near the ocean, create barriers against floods, and educate people about what to do when disasters happen.

What Can Be Done

Many of the things we need to do to fight against climate change are closely related to the other goals of the SDGs. Actively using renewable energy, such as solar or wind power, is connected with SDG 7, "Affordable and Clean Energy," and replacing regular lights with LEDs and reducing food mileage are connected with SDG 12, "Responsible Consumption and Production."

The most important measure to fight climate change is still to reduce carbon dioxide emissions as much as possible. There are many things we can do in our daily lives, such as not leaving lights on, reducing plastic waste, and walking or cycling instead of driving.

Goal 14 ···

Protect Life Below Water

••

SDG 14 is about taking care of the oceans and everything that lives in them. The oceans are important because they give us food, make half of the world's oxygen, and affect the weather. One target is to stop overfishing. If we catch too many fish, it can harm the balance of sea life. Another is to protect special areas in the ocean, like coral reefs and mangroves. These places are homes for many sea animals, and they also help keep the water clean. Reducing pollution in the oceans is another target. We need to use less plastic because it can harm sea creatures.

Seafood and Fishing

Overfishing is becoming a serious problem that

affects the global food supply. Around 33 percent of fish populations worldwide are affected by overfishing. SDG 14 asks governments to make laws and plans to make sure we catch fish sustainably so that sea life stays healthy.

One way to reduce the amount of fish that we catch in the open ocean is to use more aquaculture. Aquaculture is like farming, but in the water. Instead of growing plants on land, people raise and grow fish, shrimp, and other water creatures in special areas, like ponds or tanks. It is a way to produce seafood without relying only on catching fish from oceans and rivers. Today, aquaculture gives us about 50 percent of the fish we eat. SDG 14 encourages responsible aquaculture, making sure that we have enough fish without harming the oceans.

The Carbon Cycle

The carbon cycle is a natural system that moves carbon around the earth. Plants take in carbon dioxide from the air during photosynthesis, and animals breathe out carbon dioxide. The oceans also play a big role by taking carbon dioxide from the air and then releasing it back. However, too much carbon dioxide from human activities is causing a problem. The extra carbon dioxide in the air is raising acid levels in the ocean. This is bad for sea life, especially for creatures like corals, shellfish, and small animals. Research suggests that the ocean's acidity has increased by about 30 percent since the beginning of the Industrial Revolution.

Microplastics

Microplastics are tiny pieces of plastic that are smaller than 5 millimeters, like small beads or fibers. They often come from bigger plastic items that break down over time. These tiny plastic bits can harm sea life when they eat them. The plastic can also take in harmful chemicals, making it more dangerous. Research shows that microplastics have been found in the stomachs of many kinds of fish and sea birds. It is believed that about 8 million tons of plastic end up in the oceans every year.

SDG 14 helps deal with the microplastic problem by aiming to reduce pollution in the oceans. By stopping the use of too much plastic, especially single-use items, and improving waste management, SDG 14 helps keep our water cleaner. If we take care of the oceans and reduce our use of plastic, we can help protect sea life and make sure our planet stays healthy.

The Pacific Garbage Patch

The Pacific Garbage Patch is a big area in the Pacific Ocean where a lot of plastic and trash gather because of ocean currents. The patch is thought to be three times the size of France. Most of the trash is plastic, which takes a very long time to break down. Animals in the ocean can mistake the plastic pieces for food.

Efforts are underway to clean up the mess. Some organizations use big nets to collect the floating plastic, while others are trying to develop new technologies to make the cleanup easier. However, it is a tough job because the patch is very large and is always changing.

Preventing more plastic from getting into the ocean is also important. Many groups are working to teach people about reducing plastic use and encouraging recycling to stop more trash from getting into our oceans. It is a big challenge, but people around the world are working together to make a difference.

What Can Be Done?

Governments can create laws and rules to stop overfishing, pollution, and illegal fishing. They can also protect special areas in the ocean, like coral reefs, to keep sea life safe. Supporting and following international agreements is important so we can work together to fix problems.

You can help too. One simple thing is to use less plastic. Plastic waste harms the oceans, so using reusable bags and bottles is a good idea. Recycling also makes a difference. It is important not to throw garbage into the oceans and to pick up litter when possible. People can also support sustainable seafood by choosing fish that are caught or farmed responsibly. Being careful about what we buy and how it is made can reduce pollution and help protect the oceans. When governments and individuals work together, we can make sure the oceans stay healthy for everyone.

Goal 15 ·····················

Protect Life on Land

SDG 15 is to protect ecosystems, fix damaged ones, and make sure that they are being used sustainably. It is about taking care of the earth's land and the plants and animals that live on it.

One important target is to stop deforestation and make sure that forests are healthy. Another is to fight desertification and make sure that the soil is good for farming. It is also necessary to prevent the loss of biodiversity, which means protecting different types of plants and animals to keep the balance in nature. Other targets focus on promoting the fair and sustainable use of resources from the land and making sure that everyone has equal access to them.

Biodiversity

Biodiversity is the word we use to talk about the different kinds of living things on the earth. For example, there are many kinds of plants, animals, fungi, and bacteria. Some places have more biodiversity than others. This means they have more types of living things. Biodiversity is important for the health of our planet and for humans, too. We need biodiversity for food, medicine, clothes, and other things.

One way to protect biodiversity is to stop doing things that can harm plants and animals. For example, cutting down too many trees can be bad for the homes of many creatures. SDG 15 encourages countries to find better ways to use the land without hurting the living things that call it home.

Another way to protect biodiversity is by creating special places called reserves. These are safe zones where plants and animals can live without being disturbed. Reserves help species that might be in danger, giving them a chance to grow and live comfortably.

Deforestation and Desertification

Twenty-five percent of the world's population, or 1.6 billion people, need forests for building, heating their homes, and farming. However, the world faces a serious problem called deforestation. Although forests cover about 10 percent of the total land area in the world, it is said that about 13.7 million hectares of forest are lost every year on our planet. Loss of forests can lead to global warming, desertification, and acid rain, as well as increasing the number of large floods and landslides, so many countries are planting more trees and making laws to protect forested areas.

Desertification is a problem that happens when land becomes dry and unable to support plants. This makes it hard for people and animals to live there. When people cut down too many trees or farm the land too much, it can make the soil weak and unable to hold water. This is bad for plants and makes it easy for wind and water to take away the soil. Every year, over 4 million square kilometers of land are being turned into desert.

Biodiversity Hotspots

Biodiversity hotspots are special areas on earth with many different plants, animals, and other living things. These places have a wide variety of life, but they are also at risk of losing species. More than 70 percent of these ecosystems have already been destroyed because of things like farming, road building, and mining. Although the amount of land in biodiversity hotspots is only about 2.4 percent of the earth's total, the living things there make up between 30 and 60 percent of the plants and animals. These hotspots give us many things we need, like food, medicine, and clean air. The goal is to stop actions that harm these places, such as cutting down too many trees or taking too much from the land. Instead, we should find ways to use the land that keeps it healthy.

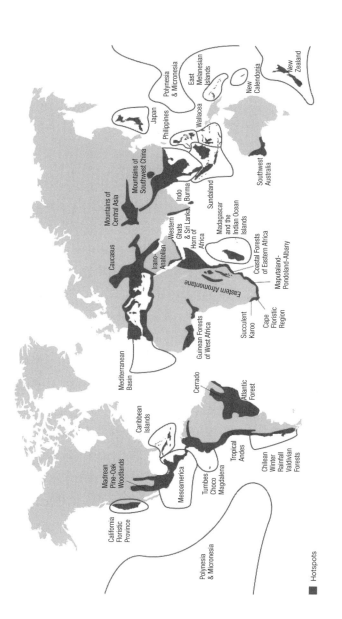

Hotspots

The Amazon Rainforest

The Amazon, the largest tropical forest on earth, covers an area of 5.5 million square kilometers. The water from the 7,000-kilometer-long Amazon River supports the rich forests, and the forests and rivers support a wide variety of ecosystems. The Amazon rainforest is called the "lungs of the earth" because it produces 20 percent of the oxygen on the planet. It also absorbs some of the carbon dioxide released by humans, so it is helping to slow global warming. The Amazon often has forest fires caused by dry weather and lightning during the dry season, and the native forests are often burned by humans to get land for raising animals or crops. From 2019 to 2020, some of the worst fires in history happened due to illegal deforestation. When tropical Amazonian forests burn, not only are ecosystems destroyed, but the jobs and cultures of the indigenous peoples who live there are also at risk.

What Can Be Done?

Wildlife, endangered species, and deforestation may not seem to have a direct effect on our daily lives. However, they are all connected. When humans harm the environment through things like illegal logging, it harms the natural balance of the earth and makes global warming worse. Governments need to make laws to stop illegal activities that harm the earth and create programs that help to fix the damage that has been done to land ecosystems.

Ordinary people can do things like making sure that wood products are not produced through illegal logging. Look for a Forest Stewardship Council label to be sure that wood products were produced in a way that did less harm to the environment. You can also donate to organizations that help with forest resource conservation or actually participate in tree-planting activities as a volunteer.

Another thing you can do is to participate in fundraising and events through organizations and companies that help to save endangered species. For example, you can visit the WWF Japan's website for information on nature- and environment-related events and volunteer opportunities.

Goal 16 ··

Peace, Justice, and Strong Institutions

··

SDG 16 is to create peaceful societies that are fair to everyone. One target is to reduce all forms of violence. This means working to make sure everyone feels safe in their communities. Another target is to end abuse, trafficking, and all forms of violence against children.

Building better institutions, such as court systems and police services, is another important part of this goal. This includes promoting good government and fighting against corruption in all its forms. The aim is to make sure that people can get the information they need and can participate in decision-making processes that affect their lives.

War

Right now, there are as many as 63 wars and other types of armed conflicts in the world. That includes 6 major and 57 minor or medium-sized ones. Most of them are disputes over land or civil wars. About 80 percent of all conflicts take place in Asia and Africa. At the end of 2021, the number of people forced to move due to conflict and persecution was about 89.3 million. Right now, 1 out of every 78 people in the world is a refugee or internally displaced person.

Child Soldiers

There are about 300,000 child soldiers in the world right now. More than one-third of child soldiers are in Africa. There are also tens of thousands in Myanmar. The average age is 14 and they belong to about 59 armed groups. About 60 percent of child soldiers are male, and 40 percent are female. Usually, the boys fight, and the girls are forced to marry men or become suicide bombers.

In some cases, children are suddenly kidnapped and forced to become soldiers. In other cases, children who are suffering from poverty due to the conflict are protected by armed groups, and as a result of the relationships they build, the children join the groups themselves. Children who become soldiers are sometime ordered to kill or badly hurt those close to them so that they get used to violence. Children who do not follow orders receive terrible punishments, such as having body parts cut off. Armies control children by making them afraid and by brainwashing them with alcohol and drugs.

UNICEF and other organizations have made efforts to make the armed groups release child soldiers, and by 2017, 65,000 children had been freed. However, sometimes there is no support to help children who used to be soldiers return to normal life, and the children go back to their lives as soldiers.

Stateless People

The UN says there are about 4.3 million state-less people in the world. Since only 96 countries know the number of stateless people living in their countries, the actual number is probably even higher. People become stateless when there is discrimination in nationality laws based on race, religion, or ethnicity, or when a country disappears because of wars or other changes in political conditions. People without a nationality usually cannot attend school, receive public services, or work. In addition, children born to stateless parents often become stateless themselves, and there is a fear that the negative cycle of statelessness will continue into the next generation. In fact, one in four children of stateless persons remains stateless.

Child Abuse

The number of cases of child abuse in Japan is increasing every year, with a record 2,174 arrests in 2021. The COVID-19 pandemic caused an

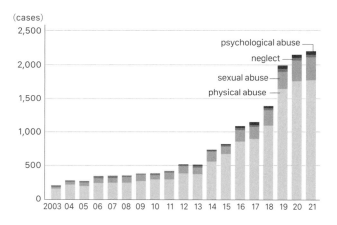

increase in school closings and remote classes, so parents and children were spending more time together at home. It seems that stress and being away from other people increased the number of child abuse cases.

Corruption

The Corruption Perceptions Index (CPI) ranks nations based on how corrupt people feel that politicians and public officials in their country are. Protecting human rights is important for fighting corruption, and countries with higher CPI scores usually have better human rights protection. The closer the CPI is to 0, the higher the level of corruption, and the closer it is to 100, the lower the level of corruption. In 2021, the average CPI was 43. Japan was ranked number 18 with a CPI score of 73. Among the least corrupt countries, Denmark, Finland, and New Zealand have the highest scores, followed by Norway, Singapore, and Sweden. On the other hand, the most corrupt country is South Sudan, followed by Syria and Somalia in second place, Venezuela in third, and Yemen and North Korea in fourth.

What Can Be Done?

Many people give donations to help sick or poor people in other countries. However, since there is a lot of corruption in some places, we must be careful about where we send our donations. If there is a lot of corruption in a country, it would be better to send donations to a third country that is providing assistance, rather than to a country directly.

In addition, we should start by taking an interest in places close to us, such as schools, companies, and our local communities. Think about what kind of problems are happening in the places where you live or work, what kind of systems are in place, what kind of solutions are available, etc. It is important to be interested in local, national, and international issues. These days, you can get a lot of information about countries around the world on the internet. If you research and gather information on your own, rather than relying only on newspapers and TV, you will be able to see things that you have not been able to see before.

Goal 17 ·····················

Achieve the Goals through Partnership

·····················

SDG 17 is the idea that countries, organizations, and people should work together to achieve the other Sustainable Development Goals. One target is to encourage international aid to help developing countries. Another target is to make global trade fair and beneficial for everyone. Also, there is a target related to technology. It must be shared so that all countries can develop.

Solving big problems, like poverty and inequality, needs everyone's effort. It is not just one country or group's job. We need to share knowledge, money, and resources. By teaming up, the world can make progress in areas that affect everyone. It is like neighbors helping each other to make their community better.

ODA and JICA

ODA means "Official Development Assistance." It is money and technical assistance for international cooperation activities by governments and various organizations that are used for development.

JICA stands for Japan International Cooperation Agency, and it is an important part of Japan's ODA program. It works with partners in Japan and abroad to create a world economy and society in which everyone can live equally, safely, and healthily while protecting the natural environment. Some of its main activities are sending technical cooperation experts to developing countries, finding volunteers to go to various countries, and bringing engineers and researchers from developing countries as trainees to provide them with knowledge and technology training.

Examples of Japanese ODA projects include improving rice farming techniques by teaching agricultural technology to Tanzanians, lending money to build a 5-kilometer-long bridge over a river in Bangladesh, and providing vaccines and equipment all over the world to stop a disease called polio.

ESGs

ESGs, or Environmental, Social, and Governance criteria, are guidelines that help companies to do good things. They help businesses make the right decisions about the environment, how they treat people, and how they will be managed. ESGs encourage companies to work together with communities, governments, and other organizations. For example, a company might think about how its actions affect the environment or if it treats its workers fairly. By following ESGs, businesses can help with the larger goal of making the world a better place for everyone. SDG 17 emphasizes the idea that we need teamwork to solve big problems, like poverty and inequality. It is about companies doing their part to create a world where everyone benefits.

What Can Be Done?

When we look at the world as a whole, we can see that these days, countries affect each other in both good and bad ways. There are many global problems related to economics, politics, society, culture, technology, and the environment. Today, we need people who know about these global problems, think globally, and take action. These individuals are called "global citizens."

Many countries are promoting global citizenship education (GCED) to teach people about being global citizens and to give them the knowledge, skills, values, and attitudes to solve international problems for a peaceful and sustainable world. In Japan, some junior high schools and universities have special programs for global citizenship education.

Being a global citizen means understanding your role as a citizen of the earth and appreciating other people, societies, and cultures. "Think globally, act locally" is a common saying, especially for environmental issues. This means that actions taken in your local area can make a difference for the whole planet. It is truly the way a global citizen thinks and acts.

SDGs Glossary

1.5 degrees
ex.) The Paris Agreement calls for countries to achieve the goal of limiting global warming to a rise of **1.5 degrees** by 2030.

4Rs
ex.) Environmentalists are encouraging people worldwide to practice the **4Rs** all the time.

absolute poverty
ex.) Many people in India live in **absolute poverty**, with no access to healthcare, potable water or proper education.

relative poverty
ex.) Many Americans are experiencing **relative poverty**, as the people rely on monthly government assistance.

abuse
ex.) The manager's treatment of his employees was a clear example of **abuse** of power.

accountable
ex.) We are **accountable** for all the environmental problems we are experiencing now.

active learning
ex.) The education ministry is encouraging teachers to use **active learning**, in which students discuss and solve problems related to current environmental issues.

adaptable
ex.) Birds can survive in many different habitats because they are **adaptable** in their eating habits.

advanced country
ex.) **Advanced countries** in Asia, like Japan, Singapore and Korea, implement strict waste disposal guidelines.

affordable

ex.) Electric cars are good for our environment but are only **affordable** to some.

afforestation

ex.) NGOs encourage schools, companies and the local community to join their **afforestation** activities.

aged

ex.) Homes for the **aged** are common in countries with a significant aging population.

aging

ex.) The **aging** population of Japan significantly affects its workforce.

super-aged

ex.) Many people in Japan and Germany are **super-aged**.

aging of society

ex.) The **aging of society** is a problem that countries like Japan, China and Korea are all experiencing.

AI, Artificial Intelligence

ex.) **AI**, or **artificial intelligence**, is gaining popularity due to Japan's lack of labor force.

alternative

ex.) **Alternative** energy sources are being developed to lessen the use of fossil fuels.

assistance

ex.) About one-fifth of the population receives **assistance** from the government.

basic living standards

ex.) None of the buildings in the slum area are even close to meeting **basic living standards**.

biocapacity

ex.) Some experts worry that humans have already exceeded the world's **biocapacity**.

biodegradable
non-biodegradable

ex.) Japan and Korea have implemented the separation of **biodegradable** and **non-biodegradable** wastes.

biodiversity

ex.) The local and international sectors aim to tackle **biodiversity** loss.

biomass

ex.) Experts are also looking into **biomass** fuels as another energy source.

black water

ex.) Water from the toilet, kitchen sink and dishwashers is categorized as **black water**.

grey water

ex.) Some building owners in Tokyo installed individual recycling or rainwater harvesting systems using **grey water**.

bluewashing

ex.) Many people see the company's new ads about its environmental commitment as an example of **bluewashing**.

greenwashing

ex.) The company's donations to the environmental group are generally seen as **greenwashing**.

bribery

ex.) It is hoped that the new law will reduce **bribery** by increasing the penalties for who are caught doing it.

bribe

ex.) Some corrupt government officials receive **bribes** from companies committing environmental offenses.

BYO

ex.) Companies and cafes have **BYO** (bring your own) programs to encourage people to help lessen plastic waste.

carbon credit

ex.) It is hoped that the use of **carbon credits** will help to reduce carbon dioxide emissions.

carbon offset

ex.) Using advanced technology to turn carbon dioxide emissions into a usable product is an example of a **carbon offset**.

carbon footprint

ex.) To reduce one's **carbon footprint**, driving electric cars is a great choice.

carbon-neutral [neutrality]

ex.) Some company buildings are attempting to become **carbon-neutral** by using solar-powered energy sources.

child mortality

ex.) Globally infectious diseases are still some countries' most significant causes of **child mortality**.

circular economy

ex.) E-cycling of used and dead batteries is an example of the **circular economy**.

class

ex.) The social **class** division in society gives unequal access to rights and resources to those at the top.

climate action

ex.) Environmental activists have been staging protests to encourage people to support **climate action**.

climate change adaptation

ex.) **Climate change adaptation** already exists as people are now more conscious and are using sustainable and renewable resources.

climate change disasters

ex.) **Climate change disasters** are more common these days.

climate change mitigation

ex.) **Climate change mitigation** is essential for the prevention of severe catastrophes.

cohousing

ex.) There are many seniors in the **cohousing** community.

combat

ex.) Various medications have been used and tested to help **combat** COVID-19.

Compact City

ex.) Hong Kong is an ultra-**compact city** with a mix of trees and an urban area co-existing simultaneously.

composting

ex.) To get started with **composting**, you first need a container to keep the waste in.

compostable

ex.) **Compostable** waste, such as food leftovers from the kitchen, is good for your garden.

conflicts

ex.) **Conflicts** among countries worldwide have become more visible because of the internet.

conserve

ex.) Driving more slowly helps to **conserve** fuel.

conservation

ex.) NGOs joined forces with the government to improve **conservation** efforts.

consumption

ex.) The **consumption** of fossil fuels is contributing to climate change.

consume

ex.) We must **consume** less so future generations can enjoy a clean environment.

coral bleaching

ex.) Climate change is the primary cause of **coral bleaching**.

corruption

ex.) **Corruption** is still a problem experienced by all countries.

cruelty-free

ex.) **Cruelty-free** products are emerging to discourage people from buying products from companies that use live animals for product testing.

cultural heritage

ex.) Italy is known for its long **cultural heritage**.

decent work

ex.) The NGO is working to increase opportunities for **decent work** among people with disabilities.

deforestation

ex.) **Deforestation** is the primary cause of the country's flash floods and landslides.

reforestation

ex.) NGOs and the government are working hand-in-hand to promote **reforestation** and solve this problem.

development

ex.) The **development** of advanced technology is a significant contributor to pollution.

digital divide

ex.) One way to overcome the **digital divide** is to provide computers to poor families.

digital transformation

ex.) Improvements in internet technology have led to **digital transformation** in many industries.

dignity

ex.) The former president was known to be a man of **dignity** with a strong persona.

disadvantage

ex.) One **disadvantage** of electric cars is that they do not have as much range as gasoline-powered vehicles.

disadvantaged

ex.) The city has launched a program to help people who are **disadvantaged** due to lack of education.

discrimination

ex.) Racial **discrimination** gave birth to the Black Lives Matter (BLM) movement.

e-cycling

ex.) These days, many batteries undergo **e-cycling** after they die.

ecolabel

ex.) **Ecolabels** are placed on products to inform consumers about how eco-friendly they are.

ecological devastation

ex.) The global economy is impacted by the **ecological devastation** caused by global warming.

ecological [nature] restoration

ex.) **Ecological restoration** programs encourage farmers to use natural fertilizers to control pests.

ecosystems

ex.) Marine **ecosystems** must be preserved and restored.

education gap

ex.) The **education gap** between men and women in the country has declined by 20 percent over the past two decades.

elimination

ex.) It is hoped that improvements in electric vehicles will someday lead to the **elimination** of gasoline-powered ones.

emissions

ex.) Electric cars produce fewer carbon **emissions** than ordinary vehicles do.

empowerment

ex.) The government believes very strongly in the **empowerment** of women.

empower

ex.) It is hoped that the new policies will help to **empower** women and minorities.

endangered [threatened] species

ex.) Many animals that are common today may become **endangered species** if the effects of global warming are not reduced.

energy conservation

ex.) We can create new appliances that promote **energy conservation** using new technology.

energy efficient

ex.) More and more companies are creating **energy-efficient** products to help lessen the effects of global warming.

equitable

ex.) **Equitable** wages will never become a reality as long as divisions between social classes exist.

equity

ex.) The NGO hopes that its work will help women to achieve **equity** in the workplace.

ESG

ex.) **ESG** (environmental, social and governance) investing is often criticized because it confuses investors.

ethical consumption

ex.) Environmentalists are encouraging everyone to practice **ethical consumption**.

ethical fashion

ex.) Many brands are introducing **ethical fashion** collections to support the fight against climate change.

fast fashion

ex.) **Fast fashion** companies are often accused of contributing to environmental problems.

slow fashion

ex.) The use of linen and organic cotton by **slow fashion** retailers helps to keep the environmental impact low.

exploitation

ex.) Child **exploitation** is still common worldwide.

extreme weather

ex.) **Extreme weather**, such as massive typhoons and hurricanes, is becoming more common.

fair trade

ex.) More and more supermarkets are selling **fair trade** products.

food mileage

ex.) Some groups are advocating that **food mileage**, or food mile labels, should be placed on products so consumers will know how far their food has traveled and how it affects the environment.

food shortage

ex.) There are still many places in Africa experiencing water and **food shortages**.

free trade

ex.) The government is confident that the new **free trade** agreement will help to reduce prices for consumers.

gender bias

ex.) Unfortunately, there is still a lot of **gender bias** that makes it difficult for women to get promoted.

gender disparities

ex.) Companies need to do more to reduce **gender disparities** in worker pay.

gender diversity

ex.) To promote **gender diversity**, the firm has been trying to recruit more female employees.

gender equality
ex.) Many women feel that the government needs to do more to promote **gender equality**.

gender inequality
ex.) **Gender inequality** is still common in many societies due to old-fashioned attitudes.

gender pay gap
ex.) The **gender pay gap** was a common problem in the past, as women were thought to be less talented than men.

geothermal
ex.) **Geothermal** energy sources are an option experts are looking into because the amount of heat generated by the Earth's core is unlimited.

global partnership
ex.) **Global partnership** is needed because we all know that "no man is an island."

global warming
ex.) **Global warming** exists because humans use and abuse the earth's natural resources.

governance
ex.) The company has promised to improve its **governance**, especially in terms of environmental responsibility.

green infrastructure
ex.) Governments are making efforts to create **green infrastructure** within the cities.

habitat
ex.) Many marine animals' **habitats** have been damaged by illegal fishing.

hate crime
ex.) The number of **hate crimes** against Asians increased during the pandemic.

health care

ex.) The COVID-19 pandemic was a huge strain on **health care** systems around the world.

human rights

ex.) People are angry because the government has violated many people's **human rights**.

human trafficking

ex.) **Human trafficking** is still common in some parts of the world.

hunger

ex.) Poverty is one of the many causes of **hunger** worldwide.

hygiene

ex.) The lack of water in African countries prevents many from being able to have proper **hygiene**.

ICT, information and communication technology

ex.) **ICT**, or **information and communication technology**, students are growing in number as the demand for jobs in the industry increases.

ICT education

ex.) Elementary students are now taught **ICT education** because of the advancement of technology.

illicit financial flows

ex.) Africa loses billions of dollars every year due to **illicit financial flows**.

illiterate

ex.) The number of **illiterate** people is still growing, even with the development of technology.

inadequate

ex.) **Inadequate** education on contraception is a major cause of teenage pregnancy.

inclusion
ex.) The company has updated its **inclusion** policy to make sure that all employees are treated fairly.

inclusive
ex.) Many shops or restaurants have gender-**inclusive** restrooms to cater to all sexes.

Industrial Revolution
ex.) Steam power and the **Industrial Revolution** transformed the world in the late 1700s.

infected
ex.) People **infected** with COVID-19 are kept isolated until their test comes out negative.

infectious
ex.) COVID-19 is the most recent **infectious** disease and has killed millions worldwide.

infrastructure
ex.) A huge amount of **infrastructure** was damaged because of the recent torrential rains and heavy floods.

internally displaced people
ex.) Many **internally displaced people** have been spread throughout the country.

international aid
ex.) **International aid** came to the country after it was hit with one of the strongest typhoons in its history.

labor
ex.) Because of the aging society in some countries, their **labor** force is decreasing.

forced labor
ex.) Human trafficking poses a lot of risks which include **forced labor**.

leading cause

ex.) The **leading cause** of death worldwide is cardiovascular disease.

LGBTQ+

ex.) Although their rights were once ignored, members of the **LGBTQ+** community have worked hard to gain acceptance in society.

life expectancy

ex.) The **life expectancy** of a man in North America is between 75 and 78 years of age, depending on where he lives.

lifelong learning

ex.) To encourage **lifelong learning**, the university has added more classes that are open to members of the local community.

literacy

ex.) English **literacy** is essential in this generation since the world is becoming globalized.

low-carbon

ex.) Electric vehicles are an important part of the **low-carbon** economy.

malnourished

ex.) One in every three children under the age of five is **malnourished**.

marine ecology

ex.) One of the most important principles of **marine ecology** is to maintain a balance in the ecosystem.

microfibers
microplastics

ex.) **Microfibers** are one example of **microplastics** that, once inhaled by humans, may affect one's health.

microorganism

ex.) Due to the COVID-19 pandemic, people are now more cautious about any **microorganisms** that they might come into contact with.

migrants

ex.) A large number of **migrants** have arrived in the city to look for work.

migration

ex.) International **migration** is popular nowadays as people search for better opportunities abroad.

modern slavery

ex.) Forcing people to work in factories for little or no pay is a form of **modern slavery**.

nature-based solutions

ex.) Land conservation and restoration are some examples of **nature-based solutions** to decrease the effects of climate change.

non-binary

ex.) People who are **non-binary** often prefer not to be referred to as "he" or "she."

non-discrimination

ex.) The right to equal treatment before the law is the main principle of equality and **non-discrimination**.

numeracy

ex.) **Numeracy** is essential nowadays due to the growing advancement of technology.

nutritious

ex.) Fruits and vegetables are far more **nutritious** when they are fresh.

ocean acidification

ex.) **Ocean acidification** is an increasing problem for the marine ecosystem.

organ harvesting

ex.) **Organ harvesting** is another example of why human trafficking is happening.

organic

ex.) **Organic** produce is often much more expensive than foods that are grown using chemicals.

overfishing

ex.) **Overfishing** is a common practice when people want to consume more protein every day.

overpopulation

ex.) One of the world's biggest problems is still **overpopulation**, as the data show there are already over eight billion people on Earth.

pandemic

ex.) The COVID-19 **pandemic** shut down borders worldwide in March 2020.

permaculture

ex.) The **permaculture** movement is still criticized even though it has introduced energy-saving green initiatives.

polluted

ex.) **Polluted** sea waters have caused various marine organisms to die.

pollution

ex.) In some cities, people have to stay indoors because the air **pollution** is so bad.

preserve

ex.) Many environmentalists aim to **preserve** nature for future generations.

preservation

ex.) The **preservation** of this forest will greatly benefit the plants and animals that live there.

prevent

ex.) All employees were asked to wear masks in order to **prevent** the spread of COVID-19.

productive

ex.) Thanks to computers, most workers have become far more **productive** in recent years.

productivity

ex.) Working from home during the pandemic caused a rise in employees' **productivity**.

QOL, Quality of Life

ex.) To enjoy a good **quality of life**, you need health and friends as well as money.

race

ex.) **Race** should never be considered when making decisions about hiring.

redistribution of wealth

ex.) Taxes are one of the most effective ways of achieving **redistribution of wealth**.

refugees

ex.) Ukrainian **refugees** have escaped to various countries for safety.

renewable energy

ex.) Consumers these days are looking for more **renewable energy** sources.

resilience

ex.) The local people showed great **resilience** after the terrible earthquake.

resilient

ex.) Some species are more **resilient** than others when their habitats are polluted.

resources

ex.) Experts are looking for more-efficient energy **resources** to help fight global warming.

responsible

ex.) Everyone is **responsible** for protecting the environment.

rural depopulation

ex.) Some areas in Japan are experiencing **rural depopulation** because most people have moved to bigger cities and the birth rate has dropped.

sanitation

ex.) Proper handwashing and **sanitation** would greatly help us lessen the spread of COVID-19.

save

ex.) The government is trying to **save** the environment by encouraging people to recycle.

sexual exploitation

ex.) **Sexual exploitation** is an ongoing problem that affects women in many countries.

sharing economy

ex.) The popularity of Airbnb is a great example of the benefits of the **sharing economy**.

social good

ex.) Healthcare, literacy and sustainable energy are all examples of **social goods**.

social protection

ex.) Pensions are an important **social protection** that help people to have financial security after they retire.

starve

ex.) Many people were left to **starve** for days when help could not reach the remote area.

struggle

ex.) Many refugees **struggle** with their new country's language.

suffer from

ex.) Patients who **suffered from** COVID-19 shared what it felt like to have the sickness.

sufficient

ex.) Recent research suggests that the COVID-19 vaccine has the potential to provide **sufficient** protection after a single dose.

sustainable

ex.) Solar energy is one of the few familiar **sustainable** energy sources.

sustainability

ex.) Environmental **sustainability** practices aim to reduce emissions, prevent pollution and waste, and reduce energy use.

sustainable industrialization

ex.) Renewable energy sources, like solar, will help us to achieve **sustainable industrialization**.

technological innovation

ex.) **Technological innovation** is essential for building a strong economy.

throw away

ex.) Many people **throw away** their used masks carelessly.

transparency

ex.) **Transparency** is what people always want from government officials.

triangular cooperation

ex.) The Philippines is the beneficiary of **triangular cooperation** in agriculture with Indonesia and Japan.

universal health coverage

ex.) Having **universal health coverage** lessens people's problems when they become ill.

urban congestion

ex.) With more people living in urban areas, **urban congestion** is becoming more serious.

urbanization

ex.) **Urbanization** has led to shrinking population in the countryside.

vegan

ex.) **Vegan** diets are becoming more popular these days.

virtual water

ex.) Many items we use every day, such as jeans, smartphones, electricity and even hamburgers, use **virtual water**.

vocational training

ex.) The Department of Education emphasizes the importance of giving **vocational training** to students.

vulnerable

ex.) Young children and senior citizens are the most **vulnerable** to COVID-19.

water security

ex.) Climate change and drastic environmental changes are causing panic over **water security**.

water shortage

ex.) **Water shortages** are a common problem following typhoons and other disasters.

water stress

ex.) **Water stress** is a significant effect of global warming.

well-being

ex.) Parents are responsible for their children's **well-being**.

work-life balance

ex.) Having a good **work-life balance** lessens a person's stress.

zero-waste

ex.) Many governments are looking for ways to become **zero-waste** countries.

Word List

□ **4Rs** 略 4R《Refuse, Reduce, Reuse, Recycle》

□ **℃ (degrees Celsius)** 略 セ氏〜度

A

□ **a lot of** たくさんの〜

□ **a number of** いくつかの〜，多くの〜

□ **ability** 名 ①できること，（〜する）能力 ②才能

□ **about** 熟 care about 〜を気に掛ける hear about 〜について聞く

□ **absolute** 形 ①完全な，絶対の ②無条件の ③確実な

□ **absolute poverty** 絶対的貧困

□ **absorb** 動 吸収する

□ **abuse** 名 虐待，悪用，乱用 child abuse 児童虐待

□ **accept** 動 ①受け入れる ②同意する，認める

□ **acceptance** 名 ①受諾，容認 ②採用，合格

□ **access** 名 ①接近，近づく方法，通路 ②（システムなどへの）アクセス

□ **accessible** 形 近づきやすい，利用できる

□ **accident** 名 ①（不慮の）事故，災難 ②偶然 traffic accident 交通事故

□ **according** 副《 – to 〜》〜によれば［よると］

□ **accountable** 形 責任がある

□ **accuse** 動《 – of 〜》〜（の理由）で告訴［非難］する

□ **achieve** 動 成し遂げる，達成する，成功を収める

□ **acid** 名 酸

□ **acid rain** 酸性雨

□ **acidification** 熟 ocean acidification 海洋の酸性化

□ **acidity** 名 酸性（度）

□ **act** 名 行為，行い 動 ①行動する ②機能する ③演じる

□ **action** 熟 climate action 気候変動に関する行動《温室効果ガスの排出を原因とする地球温暖化現象が招く世界各地での気候変動やその影響を軽減することが目標》

□ **active** 形 ①活動的な ②積極的な ③活動［作動］中の

□ **active learning** アクティブラーニング（能動的学習）

□ **actively** 副 活発に, 活動的に

□ **activist** 名 活動家, 実践主義者

□ **activity** 名 活動, 活気

□ **actual** 形 実際の, 現実の

□ **actually** 副 実際に, 本当に, 実は

□ **ad** 略 advertisement（広告, 宣伝）の略

□ **adaptable** 形 順応できる, 適応できる

□ **adaptation** 名 順応, 適応 **climate change adaptation** 気候変動適応策

□ **add** 動 ①加える, 足す ②足し算をする ③言い添える

□ **addition** 名 ①付加, 追加, 添加 ②足し算 **in addition** 加えて, さらに

□ **additional** 形 追加の, さらなる

□ **additionally** 副 その上, さらに

□ **adult** 名 大人, 成人

□ **advance** 名 進歩, 前進

□ **advanced** 形 上級の, 先に進んだ, 高等の

□ **advanced country** 先進国

□ **advancement** 名 進歩, 前進, 昇進

□ **advocate** 名 提唱者, 支持者 動 主張する, 提唱する

□ **affect** 動 ①影響する ②（病気などが）おかす ③ふりをする

□ **afford** 動《can –》～することができる, ～する（経済的・時間的な）余裕がある

□ **affordable** 形 手ごろな［良心的な］価格の,（困難などが）十分に乗り越えられる

□ **afforestation** 名 植林, 造林

□ **Afghanistan** 名 アフガニスタン《国》

□ **Africa** 名 アフリカ《大陸》 **North Africa** 北アフリカ

□ **African** 形 アフリカ（人）の

□ **again** 熟 **over and over again** 何度も繰り返して

□ **aged** 名 高齢

□ **agency** 名 ①代理店, 仲介 ②機関, 政府機関 ③媒介, 媒体

□ **aging** 名 高齢化

□ **aging of society** 高齢化社会

□ **agreed** 形 同意された

□ **agreement** 名 ①合意, 協定 ②一致 **Paris Agreement** パリ協定《2015年の国連気候変動枠組み条約締約国会議（COP21）で採択, 2016年に発効した気候変動問題に関する国際的な枠組み》

□ **agricultural** 形 農業の, 農事の

□ **agriculture** 名 農業, 農耕

□ **AI** 略 AI, 人工知能《artificial intelligence の略》

□ **aid** 名 援助（者）, 助け **food aid** 食糧援助［支援］ **international aid** 国際協力

□ **AIDS** 略 エイズ, 後天性免疫不全症候群

□ **aim** 動 ①（武器・カメラなどを）向ける ②ねらう, 目指す 名 ねらい, 目標

□ **air pollution** 空気［大気］汚染

□ **Airbnb** 名 Airbnb（エアビーアンドビー）《正式なホテルなどの宿泊施設ではなく, 世界各国の現地の人たちが, 自宅などを宿泊施設として提供するインターネット上のサービス, 及びサービスを提供する会社の名前》

□ **alcohol** 名 アルコール

□ **all over the world** 世界中に

□ **all the time** ずっと, いつも, その間ずっと

□ **allow** 動 ①許す,《– … to ～》…が～するのを可能にする, …に～させておく ②与える

□ **along with** ～と一緒に

□ **also** 熟 **not only ～ but also...** ～だけでなく…もまた

A
B
C
D
E
F
G
H
I
J
K
L
M
N
O
P
Q
R
S
T
U
V
W
X
Y
Z

□ **alternative** 名代替策, 代替手段 形別の, 代わりの

□ **although** 接〜だけれども, 〜にもかかわらず, たとえ〜でも

□ **Amazon** 名アマゾン (の熱帯雨林) **Amazon rainforest** アマゾンの熱帯雨林 **Amazon River** アマゾン川

□ **Amazonian** 形アマゾンの, アマゾン川の

□ **America** 名アメリカ《国名・大陸》 **North America** 北アメリカ, 北米 **South America** 南アメリカ (大陸)

□ **American** 形アメリカ (人) の 名アメリカ人

□ **amount** 名①量, 額 ②《the－》合計

□ **and so on** 〜など, その他もろもろ

□ **apart** 副①ばらばらに, 離れて ②別にして, それだけで

□ **app** 略アプリ

□ **appliance** 名器具, 道具, (家庭用) 電気製品

□ **appreciate** 動①正しく評価する, よさがわかる ②価値 [相場] が上がる ③ありがたく思う

□ **aquaculture** 名水産養殖

□ **armed** 形武装した, 武器を持った

□ **army** 名軍隊, 《the－》陸軍

□ **around** 熟 **move around** あちこち移動する

□ **arrest** 名逮捕

□ **arrive in** 〜に着く

□ **artificial** 形①人工的な ②不自然な, わざとらしい

□ **Artificial Intelligence** AI (人工知能)

□ **as** 熟 **as a result** その結果 (として) **as a result of** 〜の結果 (として) **as a whole** 全体として **as 〜 as possible** できるだけ〜 **as good as** 〜も同然で, ほとんど〜 **as long as** 〜する以上は, 〜である限りは **as many as** 〜もの数の **as much as** 〜と同じだけ **as well** なお, その上, 同様に **as well as** 〜と同様に **be known as** 〜として知られている **be seen as** 〜として見られる **such as** たとえば〜, 〜のような **the same 〜 as** ……と同じ (ような) 〜

□ **Asia** 名アジア **West Asia** 西アジア

□ **Asian** 名アジア人 形アジアの

□ **aspect** 名①状況, 局面, 側面 ②外観, 様子

□ **assistance** 名援助, 支援

□ **assume** 動①仮定する, 当然のことと思う ②引き受ける

□ **at a time** 一度に, 続けざまに

□ **at home** 自宅で, 在宅して

□ **at the end of** 〜の終わりに

□ **atmosphere** 名①大気, 空気 ②雰囲気

□ **attempt** 動試みる, 企てる 名試み, 企て, 努力

□ **attend** 動出席する

□ **attitude** 名姿勢, 態度, 心構え

□ **available** 形利用 [使用・入手] できる, 得られる

□ **average** 名平均 (値), 並み 形平均の, 普通の 動平均して〜になる

□ **avoid** 動避ける, (〜を) しないようにする

□ **awareness** 名認識, 自覚, 意識性, 気づいていること

□ **awareness barrier** 意識の壁

□ **away** 熟 **far away** 遠く離れて **move away from** 〜から遠ざかる **stay away from** 〜から離れている **take away** ①連れ去る ②取り上げる, 奪い去る ③取り除く **throw away** 〜を捨てる;〜を無駄に費やす, 浪費する

B

- [ ] **baby** 熟 have a baby 赤ちゃんを産む
- [ ] **back** 熟 get back 戻る, 帰る **go back to** ~に帰る[戻る], ~に遡る, (中断していた作業に)再び取り掛かる
- [ ] **background** 名 背景, 前歴, 生い立ち
- [ ] **bacteria** 名 バクテリア, 細菌
- [ ] **bad** 熟 go bad (飲食物が)腐る
- [ ] **badly** 副 ①悪く, まずく, へたに ②とても, ひどく
- [ ] **bag** 熟 eco-friendly bag 環境に優しい[配慮した]買い物袋
- [ ] **Bahamas** 名 バハマ《国名》
- [ ] **balance** 名 ①均衡, 平均, 落ち着き ②てんびん ③残高, 差額 **out of balance** 不均衡 **work-life balance** 仕事と生活の調和, ワーク・ライフ・バランス 動 釣り合いをとる
- [ ] **balanced** 形 バランス[釣り合い・均衡]の取れた
- [ ] **Bangladesh** 名 バングラデシュ《国名》
- [ ] **barrier** 名 さく, 防壁, 障害(物), 障壁 **awareness barrier** 意識の壁 **information barrier** 情報の壁 **physical barrier** 物理的な壁
- [ ] **base** 動《- on ~》~に基礎を置く, 基づく
- [ ] **basic** 形 基礎の, 基本の
- [ ] **basic living standards** 基本的生活水準
- [ ] **basketball** 名 バスケットボール
- [ ] **bathtub** 名 浴槽
- [ ] **battery** 名 電池, バッテリー
- [ ] **bead** 名 数珠玉, 《-s》ビーズ[のネックレス]
- [ ] **bean** 名 豆 **cacao bean** カカオ豆
- [ ] **because of** ~のために, ~の理由で

- [ ] **beef** 名 牛肉
- [ ] **begin with** ~で始まる
- [ ] **beginning** 名 初め, 始まり
- [ ] **belief** 名 信じること, 信念, 信用
- [ ] **belong** 動《- to ~》~に属する, ~のものである
- [ ] **below** 副 ①~より下に ②~以下の, ~より劣る
- [ ] **beneficial** 形 よい, 有益な, ためになる
- [ ] **beneficiary** 名 恩恵[利益]を受ける人.
- [ ] **benefit** 名 ①利益, 恩恵 ②(失業保険・年金などの)手当, 給付(金) 動 利益を得る, (~の)ためになる
- [ ] **bias** 名 偏見, 先入見, バイアス **gender bias** 性差別, 性差に関する偏見
- [ ] **big data** ビッグデータ《人間では全体を把握することが困難な巨大なデータ群のこと》
- [ ] **billion** 形 10億の, ばく大な, 無数の 名 10億
- [ ] **bio toilet** 名 バイオトイレ《人間の排せつ物を微生物の働きによって分解・処理するトイレ》
- [ ] **biocapacity** 名 バイオキャパシティ《ある地域, あるいは地球全体の生態系が供給できる資源の量》
- [ ] **biodegradable** 形 生(物)分解性の, 生(物)分解可能な
- [ ] **biodiversity** 名 種[生態系]の多様性, 生物学的多様性
- [ ] **Biodiversity hotspot** 生物多様性ホットスポット《地球規模での生物多様性が高いにもかかわらず, 人類による破壊の危機に瀕している地域》
- [ ] **bioenergy** 名 バイオエネルギー《動植物などの生物からつくり出されるエネルギー資源のうち, 石油などの化石燃料を除いたもの》
- [ ] **biomass** 名 バイオマス《代替エネルギーの供給源としての植物》

□ **biosphere** 名生物圏《水中・地殻中・大気中の生物が生息し得る範囲》

□ **birth** 名①出産, 誕生 ②生まれ, 起源, (よい)家柄 **give birth to ~**を生む

□ **bit** 名小片, 少量 **plastic bit** 小さなプラスチック片, マイクロプラスチック

□ **Black Lives Matter** ブラック・ライブズ・マター《黒人に対する暴力や人種差別に抗議する運動, またはその合言葉》

□ **black water** 《工場やトイレなどから出る》汚水, 下水

□ **bleaching** 名白化, 脱色, 漂白 **coral bleaching** サンゴ白化現象

□ **BLM** 略 Black Lives Matterの略《黒人に対する暴力や人種差別に抗議する運動, またはその合言葉》

□ **bluewashing** 名ブルーウォッシング《企業や政府組織が広報・経済的利益目的で見せかけの人道支援を行うこと》

□ **boiled** 形煮沸した

□ **Bolivia** 名ボリビア《国名》

□ **bomber** 名爆撃機, 爆弾投下兵

□ **border** 名境界, へり, 国境 **Doctors Without Borders** 国境なき医師団《世界75の国と地域で活動する, 民間で非営利の医療・人道援助団体》

□ **boring** 形うんざりさせる, 退屈な

□ **both A and B** AもBも

□ **bottom** 形底の, 根底の

□ **brainwash** 動洗脳する, 思想改造する

□ **brand** 名ブランド, 商標, 品種

□ **breathe** 動①呼吸する ②ひと息つく, 休息する **breathe out** 息を吐き出す

□ **bribe** 動賄賂を贈る 名賄賂

□ **bribery** 名贈収賄

□ **building** 名建物, 建造物, ビルデ

ィング

□ **burned** 形焼けた, 燃えた, 黒焦げになった

□ **but** 熟 not ~ but … ~ではなくて … not only ~ but also … ~だけでなく…もまた

□ **by** 熟 by oneself 一人で, 自分だけで, 独力で followed by その後に~が続いて

□ **BYO** 略 Bring Your Own (各自持参のこと)の略

C

□ **C** 略 セ氏 ℃ (=degrees Celsius) セ氏~度

□ **cacao** 名カカオ **cacao bean** カカオ豆

□ **cafe** 名①コーヒー[喫茶]店, 軽食堂 ②酒場

□ **cake** 熟 SDG wedding cake SDGsウェディングケーキ《気候変動や海洋汚染, 貧困問題などの社会問題解決に向けて定められた17の目標を「生物圏 (Biosphere)」「社会圏 (Society)」「経済圏 (Economy)」の3つの層に分類したもの》

□ **call** 熟 call for ~を求める, 訴える, ~を呼び求める, 呼び出す **call to ~**に声をかける

□ **camp** 名①野営(地), キャンプ ②収容所 **refugee camp** 難民キャンプ, 難民収容所

□ **Canada** 名カナダ《国名》

□ **cancer** 名癌

□ **car** 熟 self-driving car 自動運転車

□ **carbon** 名炭素

□ **carbon credit** 炭素クレジット, カーボンクレジット《先進国間で温暖化ガスの排出削減量を排出枠として売買可能にする仕組み》

□ **carbon cycle** 炭素循環《人間による化石燃料の燃焼とそれによる二酸化炭素の大気への排出を含めた, 地

球上の炭素の排出, 吸収のメカニズム
の循環系》

- [ ] **carbon dioxide** 二酸化炭素, 炭酸ガス

- [ ] **carbon footprint** カーボンフットプリント《商品やサービスのライフサイクル全体で排出される温室効果ガスの排出量をCO_2排出量に換算して表示したもの》

- [ ] **carbon monoxide** 一酸化炭素

- [ ] **carbon offset** 炭素オフセット, カーボンオフセット《炭素クレジットを購入することで排出量の一部を相殺すること》

- [ ] **carbon-neutral [neutrality]** 形 カーボンニュートラルな《二酸化炭素の排出量と吸収量のバランスが取れている》名 カーボンニュートラル《二酸化炭素プラスマイナスゼロ》

- [ ] **cardiovascular** 形 心臓血管の

- [ ] **care** 熟 care about ～を気に掛ける care to ～したいと思う health care (system) 健康保険制度 nursing care 看護, 介護 take care of ～の世話をする, ～の面倒を見る, ～を管理する

- [ ] **career** 名 ①(生涯の・専門的な) 職業 ②経歴, キャリア

- [ ] **carelessly** 副 不注意にも, ぞんざいに

- [ ] **cargo** 名 積み荷

- [ ] **cargo ship** 貨物船

- [ ] **case** 熟 in the case of ～の場合は

- [ ] **catastrophe** 名 大惨事, 大災害, 大事故

- [ ] **categorize** 動 分類する, 類別する

- [ ] **cater** 動 ①(料理などを) 提供する ②要求などを満たす

- [ ] **cause** 熟 leading cause 主要因

- [ ] **cautious** 形 用心深い, 慎重な

- [ ] **central** 形 中央の, 主要な

- [ ] **certain** 形 ①確実な, 必ず～する ②(人が) 確信した ③ある ④いくら

かの

- [ ] **challenge** 名 ①挑戦 ②難関

- [ ] **change** climate change adaptation 気候変動適応策 climate change disasters 気候変動災害 climate change mitigation 気候変動緩和策 climate change refugee 気候変動避難民《気候変動や, それによる災害で避難を余儀なくされた人々》

- [ ] **charcoal** 名 木炭

- [ ] **chart** 名 表, 図表, カルテ pie chart 円グラフ, 分円図

- [ ] **cheaply** 副 安く, 安っぽく

- [ ] **check** 動 ①照合する, 検査する ②阻止 [妨害] する ③(所持品を) 預ける

- [ ] **check-up** 名 健康診断, 健診, 検査

- [ ] **chemical** 名 化学製品 [薬品]

- [ ] **chemistry** 名 ①化学, 化学的性質, 化学反応 ②相性

- [ ] **child abuse** 児童虐待

- [ ] **child mortality** 小児死亡率

- [ ] **childcare** 名 育児, 保育

- [ ] **China** 名 ①中国《国名》②《c-》陶磁器, 瀬戸物

- [ ] **chocolate** 名 チョコレート

- [ ] **choice** 名 選択(の範囲・自由), えり好み, 選ばれた人 [物]

- [ ] **chronic** 形 (病気が) 慢性の

- [ ] **chronic hunger** 慢性飢餓《貧困や不平等, 農業生産力の低さなどの構造的な問題によって, 長期間にわたって十分な食料を得られない状態》

- [ ] **circular** 形 ①円形の, 丸い ②循環の, 周遊の 名 回状

- [ ] **circular economy** 循環型経済, サーキュラー・エコノミー《廃棄物の発生を最小限にする経済システム》

- [ ] **citizen** 名 ①市民, 国民 ②住民, 民間人

- [ ] **citizenship** 名 公民権, 市民権

141

□ **city** 熟 **compact city** コンパクトシティ《住まい・交通・公共サービス・商業施設などの生活機能をコンパクトに集約し, 効率化した都市》**smart city** スマートシティ《デジタル技術を活用して, 都市インフラ・施設や運営業務等を最適化し, 企業や生活者の利便性・快適性の向上を目指す都市》**Woven City** ウーブン・シティ《トヨタ自動車による, AI (人工知能), 自動運転技術, ロボットなどを導入した実験都市プロジェクト》

□ **civil** 形 ①一般人の, 民間 (人) の ②国内の, 国家の ③礼儀正しい

□ **civil war** 内戦, 内乱

□ **class** 名 階級

□ **cleaning** 名 掃除, クリーニング, 洗濯

□ **cleanup** 名 大掃除, 一掃, 浄化

□ **clear** 形 ①はっきりした, 明白な ②澄んだ ③(よく) 晴れた

□ **climate** 名 気候, 風土, 環境

□ **climate action** 気候変動に具体的な対策を《温室効果ガスの排出を原因とする地球温暖化現象が招く世界各地での気候変動やその影響を軽減することが目標》

□ **climate change adaptation** 気候変動適応策

□ **climate change disasters** 気候変動災害

□ **climate change mitigation** 気候変動緩和策

□ **climate change refugee** 気候変動避難民《気候変動や, それによる災害で避難を余儀なくされた人々》

□ **close to** 《be –》～に近い **be close to extinction** 絶滅の危機にひんしている

□ **closely** 副 ①密接に ②念入りに, 詳しく ③ぴったりと

□ **closing** 名 (会社・工場・施設などの) 閉鎖

□ **clothing** 名 衣類, 衣料品

□ **cm** 略 センチメートル《centimeter の略》

□ **coal** 名 石炭, 木炭

□ **co-existing** 形 共存する, (同一場所に) 同時に存在する

□ **cohousing** 名 共同住宅地《住居者が共同で施設を所有・管理する助け合いの住み方》

□ **collection** 名 収集, 収蔵物

□ **collective** 形 ①集合的な, 集団的な ②共通の

□ **colony** 名 植民 [移民] (地)

□ **combat** 動 (犯罪, 問題など) ～と闘う, (～の治療に) 効く

□ **come into** ～に入ってくる

□ **come out** 出てくる, 出掛ける, 姿を現す, 発行される

□ **come up with** ～に追いつく, ～を思いつく, 考え出す, 見つけ出す

□ **comfort** 名 ①快適さ, 満足 ②慰め ③安楽

□ **comfortable** 形 快適な, 心地いい

□ **comfortably** 副 心地よく, くつろいで

□ **commit** 動 ①委託する ②引き受ける ③(罪などを) 犯す

□ **commitment** 名 委託, 約束, 確約, 責任

□ **communication** 名 伝えること, 伝導, 連絡 **information and communication technology** 情報通信技術

□ **community** 名 ①団体, 共同社会, 地域社会 ②《the –》社会 (一般), 世間 ③共有, 共同世界

□ **compact** 形 ①ぎっしり詰まった ②小ぢんまりした, コンパクトな

□ **compact city** コンパクトシティ《住まい・交通・公共サービス・商業施設などの生活機能をコンパクトに集約し, 効率化した都市》

□ **compare** 動 ①比較する, 対照す

142

る ②たとえる

□ **completely** 副 完全に, すっかり

□ **compostable** 形 堆肥化可能な

□ **composting** 名 堆肥化

□ **concept** 名 ①概念, 観念, テーマ ②(計画案などの) 基本的な方向

□ **concrete** 名 コンクリート

□ **condition** 名 ①(健康) 状態, 境遇 ②《-s》状況, 様子 ③条件

□ **confidence** 名 自信, 確信, 信頼, 信用度

□ **confident** 形 自信のある, 自信に 満ちた

□ **conflict** 名 ①不一致, 衝突 ②争い, 対立, 紛争 ③論争 動 衝突する, 矛盾 する

□ **confuse** 動 混同する, 困惑させる, 混乱させる

□ **congestion** 名 密集, 混雑, 過密 **urban congestion** 都市過密化

□ **connected** 形 結合した, 関係のあ る

□ **connection** 名 ①つながり, 関係 ②縁故

□ **conscious** 形 ①(状況などを) 意 識している, 自覚している ②意識の ある 名 意識

□ **conservation** 名 保護, 保管, 保 存 **energy conservation** 省エネ, エ ネルギー保存

□ **conserve** 動 保護する, 保全する

□ **consider** 動 ①考慮する, ～しよう と思う ②(～と) みなす ③気にかけ る, 思いやる

□ **consideration** 名 ①考慮, 考察 ②考慮すべきこと

□ **considered** 形 考えられた, 熟考 された

□ **construct** 動 建設する, 組み立て る

□ **construction** 名 構造, 建設, 工事, 建物

□ **consume** 動 消費する

□ **consumer** 名 消費者

□ **consumption** 名 消費 (量[高]) **ethical consumption** エシカル消費 《人・社会・地域・環境などに配慮し た消費行動》

□ **contain** 動 ①含む, 入っている ② (感情などを) 抑える

□ **container** 名 ①容器, 入れ物 ② (輸送用) コンテナ

□ **contamination** 名 汚染, 汚濁

□ **contraception** 名 避妊 (法)

□ **contract** 名 契約 (書), 協定

□ **contribute** 動 ①貢献する ②寄 稿する ③寄付する

□ **contributor** 名 寄付者, 貢献者, 寄稿者

□ **control** 動 ①管理[支配]する ② 抑制する, コントロールする

□ **convenience** 名 便利 (さ), 便利 なもの, 利便性

□ **convenient** 形 便利な, 好都合な

□ **cooking** 名 料理 (法), クッキング

□ **cooking stove** 料理用コンロ

□ **cooperation** 名 ①協力, 協 業, 協調 ②協同組合 **triangular cooperation** 三角協力《開発支援に おいて途上国間の協力に先進国が加 わること》

□ **COP** 略 締約国会議《Conference of the Parties の略》

□ **COP16** 略 国連気候変動枠組条約 第16回締約国会議《2010年11月29日 -12月10日, カンクン (メキシコ)》

□ **COP21** 略 国連気候変動枠組条約 第21回締約国会議《2015年11月30日 -12月11日, パリ》

□ **coral** 名 サンゴ (珊瑚)

□ **coral bleaching** サンゴ白化現 象

□ **coral reef** サンゴ礁

□ **core** 名 核心, 中心, 芯

A
B
C
D
E
F
G
H
I
J
K
L
M
N
O
P
Q
R
S
T
U
V
W
X
Y
Z

□ **coronavirus** 名 コロナウイルス

□ **corporation** 名 法人，(株式) 会社，公団，社団法人

□ **corrupt** 形 ①堕落した ②不純な ③不正な

□ **corruption** 名 汚職，不正行為

□ **Corruption Perceptions Index (CPI)** 腐敗認識指数《世界各地の公務員と政治家が，どの程度汚職していると認識できるか，その度合を国際比較し，国家別に順位付けしたもの》

□ **cost** 名 ①値段，費用 ②損失，犠牲 動 (金・費用が) かかる，(～を) 要する，(人に金額を) 費やさせる

□ **cotton** 名 ①綿，綿花 ②綿織物，綿糸

□ **council** 名 会議，評議会，議会

□ **country** 熟 advanced country 先進国 developed country 先進国 developing country 発展 [開発] 途上国，新興国 third country 第三国

□ **countryside** 名 地方，田舎

□ **course** 熟 of course もちろん，当然

□ **court** 名 ①中庭，コート ②法廷，裁判所 ③宮廷，宮殿

□ **court system** 裁判制度

□ **cover** 動 ①覆う，包む，隠す ②扱う，(～に) わたる，及ぶ ③代わりを務める ④補う

□ **coverage** 名 ①取材範囲，報道 ②保険による保護，適用 [通用] 範囲 universal health coverage 国民保険制度

□ **COVID-19** 略 新型コロナウイルス感染症《coronavirus disease 2019 の略》

□ **CPI** 略 腐敗認識指数《Corruption Perceptions Index の略》

□ **create** 動 創造する，生み出す，引き起こす

□ **creation** 名 創造 [物]

□ **creative** 形 創造力のある，独創的な

□ **creature** 名 (神の) 創造物，生物，動物 sea creature 海の生き物，海獣

□ **credit** 名 ①信用，評判，名声 ②掛け売り，信用貸し **carbon credit** 炭素クレジット，カーボンクレジット《先進国間で温暖化ガスの排出削減量を排出枠として売買可能にする仕組み》

□ **crime** 名 ①(法律上の) 罪，犯罪 ②悪事，よくない行為 hate crime ヘイトクライム，憎悪犯罪

□ **criteria** 名 基準《criterion の複数形》

□ **criticize** 動 ①非難する，あら探しをする ②酷評する ③批評する

□ **crop** 名 作物，収穫

□ **cruelty-free** 形 動物実験を行っていない

□ **cultural** 形 文化の，文化的な

□ **cultural heritage** 文化遺産

□ **cure** 名 治療，治癒，矯正

□ **current** 形 現在の，目下の，通用 [流通] している 名 流れ，電流，風潮

□ **currently** 副 今のところ，現在

□ **customer** 名 顧客

□ **cut down trees** 木を伐採する

□ **cut off** 切断する，切り離す

□ **cycle** 名 ①周期，循環 ②自転車，オートバイ **carbon cycle** 炭素循環《人間による化石燃料の燃焼とそれによる二酸化炭素の大気への排出を含めた，地球上の炭素の排出，吸収のメカニズムの循環系》 **poverty cycle** 貧困の循環

□ **cycling** 名 サイクリング

D

□ **daily** 形 毎日の，日常の

□ **damage** 名 損害，損傷

□ **damaged** 形 損傷した，傷んだ，壊れた

144

□ **data** 图 データ, 情報 **big data** ビッグデータ《人間では全体を把握することが困難な巨大なデータ群のこと》

□ **day** 熟 **every day** 毎日 **these days** このごろ

□ **deal** 動 ①分配する ②《 – with [in] ～》～を扱う

□ **death** 图 ①死, 死ぬこと ②《the – 》終えん, 消滅

□ **decade** 图 10年間

□ **decent** 形 ①きちんとした, 礼儀正しい, 上品な ②まあまあの ③親切な

□ **decent work** ディーセントワーク《働きがいのある人間らしい仕事》

□ **decision** 图 ①決定, 決心 ②判決

□ **decision-making** 图 意思［政策・対策］決定

□ **decline** 動 ①断る ②傾く ③衰える 图 ①傾くこと ②下り坂, 衰え, 衰退

□ **decrease** 動 減少する 图 減少

□ **deeply** 副 深く, 非常に

□ **defecate** 動 排便する

□ **deforestation** 图 森林伐採

□ **degree** 图 ①程度, 階級, 位, 身分 ②（温度・角度の）度 **1.5 degrees** 1.5度（目標）

□ **deliver** 動 ①配達する, 伝える ②達成する, 果たす

□ **demand** 動 ①要求する, 尋ねる ②必要とする 图 ①要求, 請求 ②需要

□ **democracy** 图 民主主義, 民主政治

□ **Denmark** 图 デンマーク《国名》

□ **department** 图 ①部門, 課, 局, 担当分野 ②《D-》（米国・英国の）省

□ **depend** 動 《 – on [upon] ～》①～を頼る, ～をあてにする ②～による

□ **dependent** 形 頼っている, ～次第である

□ **depopulated** 形 人口が減少した, 過疎の

□ **depopulation** 图 人口（の）減少, 過疎（化） **rural depopulation** 農村部の人口減少

□ **deportation** 图 （外国人の）国外退去

□ **desert** 图 砂漠, 不毛の地

□ **desertification** 图 砂漠化

□ **designer** 图 デザイナー, 設計者

□ **destroy** 動 破壊する, 絶滅させる, 無効にする

□ **detergent** 图 合成洗剤, 洗剤

□ **devastation** 图 破壊すること, 荒廃 **ecological devastation** 生態［環境］破壊

□ **develop** 動 ①発達する［させる］②開発する

□ **developed** 形 発展した, 先進の, 成熟した

□ **developed country** 先進国

□ **developing** 形 発展［開発］途上の

□ **developing country** 発展［開発］途上国, 新興国

□ **development** 图 ①発達, 発展 ②開発 **sustainable development** 持続可能な開発

□ **device** 图 ①工夫 ②案 ③装置

□ **diabetes** 图 糖尿病

□ **diarrhea** 图 下痢

□ **diet** 图 ①食べ物, 食事 ②食習慣 ③ダイエット, 食餌療法

□ **difficulty** 图 ①むずかしさ ②難局, 支障, 苦情, 異議 ③《-ties》財政困難

□ **dig** 動 ①掘る ②小突く ③探る

□ **digital** 形 ①数字の, 数字表示の, デジタルの ②指の, 指状の

□ **digital divide** デジタル・ディバイド, デジタル格差《インターネット等の情報通信技術（ICT）を利用できる者と利用できない者との間にもたらされる格差のこと》

A
B
C
D
E
F
G
H
I
J
K
L
M
N
O
P
Q
R
S
T
U
V
W
X
Y
Z

□ **digital transformation** デジタル変革, デジタル・トランスフォーメーション《最新のデジタル技術の活用によってさまざまな分野でより便利に進化すること》

□ **dignity** 名 尊厳

□ **dioxide** 名 二酸化物 **carbon dioxide** 二酸化炭素, 炭酸ガス

□ **direct** 形 まっすぐな, 直接の, 率直な, 露骨な

□ **directly** 副 ①じかに ②まっすぐに ③ちょうど

□ **dirty** 形 ①汚い, 汚れた ②卑劣な, 不正な

□ **disability** 名 ①無力 ②身体障害

□ **disadvantage** 名 不利な状況, デメリット

□ **disadvantaged** 形 (経済的・社会的に) 恵まれない

□ **disappear** 動 見えなくなる, 姿を消す, なくなる

□ **disaster** 名 災害, 災難, まったくの失敗 **climate change disasters** 気候変動災害 **natural disaster** 自然災害, 天災

□ **discourage** 動 ①やる気をそぐ, 失望させる ②(〜するのを) 阻止する, やめさせる

□ **discriminate** 動 ①見分ける, 識別する, 区別する ②差別する

□ **discrimination** 名 差別, 区別, 識別

□ **discuss** 動 議論[検討]する

□ **disease** 名 ①病気 ②(社会や精神の) 不健全な状態 **lifestyle diseases** 生活習慣病

□ **disease-carrying** 形 病気を媒介する

□ **dishwasher** 名 食器洗浄機

□ **disparity** 格差, 不均衡 **gender disparities** ジェンダー格差, 男女間格差

□ **displaced** 形 追放された, 住むところがなくなった

□ **displaced person** 強制移住者, 難民 **internally displaced person** 国内避難民

□ **disposal** 名 処分, 廃棄 **waste disposal** 廃棄物処理

□ **dispose** 動 ①処理する, 捨てる ②配置する

□ **dispute** 名 論争, 議論

□ **disrespect** 名 軽視, 敬意の欠如

□ **distance** 名 距離, 隔たり, 遠方

□ **distribution** 名 ①分配 ②配布, 配給 ③流通 ④分布, 区分

□ **disturbed** 形 ①神経症の, 精神障害の ②かき乱された, 動揺した, 不安な

□ **diversity** 名 多様性, 相違 **gender diversity** ジェンダーの多様性

□ **divide** 動 分かれる, 分ける, 割れる, 割る **be divided into** 分けられる **divide into** 〜に分かれる 名 分割, 分裂 **digital divide** デジタル・ディバイド, デジタル格差《インターネット等の情報通信技術 (ICT) を利用できる者と利用できない者との間にもたらされる格差のこと》

□ **division** 名 ①分割 ②部門 ③境界 ④割り算

□ **do one's part** 自分の役割を果たす

□ **do well** 〜がうまくいく, 成功する

□ **Doctors Without Borders** 国境なき医師団《世界75の国と地域で活動する, 民間で非営利の医療・人道援助団体》

□ **document** 名 文書, 記録

□ **dome** 名 丸屋根, ドーム **Tokyo Dome** 東京ドーム《東京都文京区後楽にあるドーム球場。面積: 0.047 km²》

□ **domestic** 形 ①家庭の ②国内の, 自国の, 国産の

□ **domestic violence** ドメスティック・バイオレンス, 家庭内暴力

146

- □ **donate** 動寄付する，贈与する
- □ **donated** 形寄付された
- □ **donation** 名寄付金，献金
- □ **don't have to** 〜する必要はない
- □ **dose** 名（薬剤の）1回の服用量
- □ **down** 熟cut down trees 木を伐採する **go down** 下に降りる **slow down** 速度を落とす
- □ **drastic** 形強烈な，徹底した
- □ **drinking** 名飲むこと，飲酒
- □ **drinking water** 飲料水，飲用水
- □ **drive** 熟food drive フードドライブ《家庭で余っている未開封の食品を持ち寄り，フードバンクや地域の福祉施設などに寄付する活動》
- □ **driving** 名運転
- □ **drought** 名ひでり，かんばつ
- □ **drug** 名薬，麻薬，麻酔薬
- □ **due** 形予定された，期日のきている，支払われるべき **due to** 〜によって，〜が原因で
- □ **dysentery** 名赤痢

E

- □ **each one** 各自
- □ **earn** 動①儲ける，稼ぐ ②（名声を）博す
- □ **earth** 熟on earth 地球上で，この世で
- □ **earthquake** 名地震，大変動
- □ **easily** 副①容易に，たやすく，苦もなく ②気楽に
- □ **eco-friendly** 形環境［生態系］に優しい
- □ **eco-friendly bag** 環境に優しい［配慮した］買い物袋
- □ **ecolabel** 名エコラベル
- □ **ecological** 形生態学の，環境保護の
- □ **ecological devastation** 生態

［環境］破壊

- □ **ecological [nature] restoration** 生態［自然］回復
- □ **ecology** 名生態学，生態，環境，エコロジー **marine ecology** 海洋生態学
- □ **economic** 形経済学の，経済上の
- □ **economy** 名①経済，財政 ②節約 **circular economy** 循環型経済，サーキュラー・エコノミー《廃棄物の発生を最小限にする経済システム》 **sharing economy** シェアリングエコノミー，共有型経済《個人が保有する物やスキル，サービスをインターネットを介して提供したり共有したりする仕組み》
- □ **ecosystem** 名生態系，エコシステム
- □ **e-cycling** 名電子機器のリサイクル
- □ **educate** 動教育する，（〜するように）訓練する
- □ **education** 名教育，教養 **ICT education** ICT教育《パソコンやタブレット端末，インターネットなどの情報通信技術を用いた教育手法》
- □ **education gap** 教育格差
- □ **educational** 形教育（上）の
- □ **effect** 名①影響，効果，結果 ②実施，発効
- □ **effective** 形効果的である，有効である
- □ **effectively** 副効果的に，効率的に
- □ **efficient** 熟energy efficient エネルギー効率の良い
- □ **effort** 名努力（の成果）
- □ **elderly** 形かなり年配の，初老の 名《the－》お年寄り
- □ **electric** 形電気の，電動の
- □ **electricity** 名電気
- □ **elementary** 形①初歩の ②単純な，簡単な
- □ **eliminate** 動削除［排除・除去］す

147

る，撤廃する

□ **elimination** 名 削除，排除，撤廃

□ **emerge** 動 現れる，浮かび上がる，明らかになる

□ **emergency** 名 非常時，緊急時

□ **emission** 名 ①放出，放射，発射，発光，排気 ②（複数形で）排出物

□ **emotionally** 副 感情的に，情緒的に

□ **emphasize** 動 ①強調する ②重視する

□ **employee** 名 従業員，会社員，被雇用者

□ **employment** 名 ①雇用 ②仕事，職

□ **empower** 動 権限・力を与える

□ **empowerment** 名 （女性の）社会的地位の向上

□ **encourage** 動 ①勇気づける ②促進する，助長する

□ **end** 熟 at the end of ～の終わりに end up 結局～になる in the end とうとう，結局，ついに

□ **endangered** 形 危険にさらされた

□ **endangered [threatened] species** 絶滅危惧種 endangered wildlife species 絶滅のおそれのある野生生物種

□ **endless** 形 終わりのない，無限の

□ **energy** 熟 energy conservation 省エネ，エネルギー保存 energy efficient エネルギー効率の良い renewable energy 再生可能エネルギー

□ **energy-efficient** 形 エネルギー［資源］効率の良い，燃費（効率）の良い

□ **energy-saving** 形 省エネ（型）の

□ **engineer** 名 技師

□ **enough of** ～はもうたくさん

□ **enough to do** ～するのに十分な

□ **entertainment** 名 ①楽しみ，娯楽 ②もてなし，歓待

□ **entire** 形 全体の，完全な，まったくの

□ **environment** 名 ①環境 ②周囲（の状況），情勢

□ **environmental** 形 ①環境の，周囲の ②環境保護の

□ **Environmental, Social, and Governance** ESG（環境・社会・ガバナンス）《企業の持続可能性を評価する際に使われる3つの基準》

□ **environmentalist** 名 環境保護主義者

□ **environment-related** 形 環境関連の

□ **equal** 形 等しい，均等な，平等な

□ **equal opportunity** 〔雇用の〕機会均等

□ **equality** 名 平等，等しいこと gender equality 男女平等，ジェンダーの平等

□ **equally** 副 等しく，平等に

□ **equipment** 名 装置，機材，道具，設備

□ **equitable** 形 公平な，公正な

□ **equity** 名 公平，公正

□ **escape** 動 逃げる，免れる，もれる

□ **ESG** 略 ESG（環境・社会・ガバナンス）《企業の持続可能性を評価する際に使われる3つの基準。環境（E: Environment），社会（S: Social），ガバナンス（G: Governance）の英語の頭文字を合わせた言葉》

□ **essential** 形 本質的な，必須の

□ **estimate** 動 ①見積もる ②評価する

□ **estimated** 形 見積もりの，だいたいの

□ **etc** 略 ～など，その他（= et cetera）

□ **ethical** 形 倫理の，道徳的な

□ **ethical consumption** エシカ

ル消費《人・社会・地域・環境などに配慮した消費行動》

□ **ethical fashion** エシカル・ファッション《環境などに配慮した衣料品》

□ **ethnicity** 名 民族性, 民族集団

□ **Europe** 名 ヨーロッパ

□ **European** 名 ヨーロッパ人 形 ヨーロッパ(人)の

□ **evacuate** 動 ①避難する［させる］②排出する, 排泄する

□ **even if** たとえ〜でも

□ **even though** 〜であるけれども, 〜にもかかわらず

□ **every** 熟 every day 毎日 one out of every 〜 人に１人

□ **everyday** 形 毎日の, 日々の

□ **everyone** 代 誰でも, 皆

□ **everything** 代 すべてのこと［もの］, 何でも, 何もかも

□ **everywhere** 副 どこにいても, いたるところに

□ **evidence** 名 ①証拠, 証人 ②形跡

□ **example** 熟 for example たとえば

□ **exceed** 動 (程度・限度などを)超える, 上回る, 勝る

□ **excrement** 名 排せつ物

□ **exercise** 動 ①運動する, 練習する ②影響を及ぼす

□ **exhaust** 名 排気, 排出

□ **exhaust gas** 排(出)ガス

□ **exist** 動 存在する, 生存する, ある, いる

□ **existing** 形 現存の, 現在の, 現行の

□ **expand** 動 ①広げる, 拡張［拡大］する ②発展させる, 拡充する

□ **expect** 動 予期［予測］する, (当然のこととして)期待する

□ **expectancy** 名 期待, 見込み life

expectancy 平均寿命

□ **expert** 名 専門家, 熟練者, エキスパート 形 熟練した, 専門の

□ **exploitation** 名 搾取, 利己的な目的での利用 sexual exploitation 性的搾取

□ **express** 動 表現する, 述べる

□ **extinction** 名 絶滅, 死滅 be close to extinction 絶滅の危機にひんしている

□ **extra** 形 余分の, 臨時の

□ **extreme** 形 極端な, 極度の, いちばん端の

□ **extreme weather** 異常気象

□ **extremely** 副 非常に, 極度に

F

□ **facility** 名 ①(-ties)施設, 設備 ②器用さ, 容易さ

□ **fact** 熟 in fact つまり, 実は, 要するに

□ **factory** 名 工場, 製造所

□ **fair** 形 ①正しい, 公平［正当］な ②快晴の ③色白の, 金髪の ④かなりの ⑤《古》美しい

□ **fair trade** フェアトレード《農産物などを買う際に, 生産者が適切な収入を得られるように適正価格を支払う運動》

□ **fairly** 副 ①公平に ②かなり, 相当に

□ **Fairtrade** 名 国際フェアトレード認証

□ **fairness** 名 公平さ, 公明正大さ

□ **familiar** 形 ①親しい, 親密な ②《be - with 〜》〜に精通している ③普通の, いつもの, おなじみの

□ **far** 熟 how far どのくらいの距離か

□ **far away** 遠く離れて

□ **far-away place** 遠隔地

□ **farmer** 名 農民, 農場経営者

□ **farming** 名農業, 農作業

□ **fashion** 名①流行, 方法, はやり ②流行のもの (特に服装) **ethical fashion** エシカル・ファッション《環境などに配慮した衣料品》**fast fashion** ファストファッション《短いサイクルで流行のデザインを変えながら衣料品を大量生産し, 低価格で販売すること》**slow fashion** スローファッション《人権・環境・動物などに配慮した衣料品》

□ **fast fashion** ファストファッション《短いサイクルで流行のデザインを変えながら衣料品を大量生産し, 低価格で販売すること》

□ **fear** 名①恐れ ②心配, 不安

□ **feel like** ～がほしい, ～したい気がする, ～のような感じがする

□ **feeling** 名①感じ, 気持ち ②触感, 知覚 ③同情, 思いやり, 感受性

□ **female** 形女性の, 婦人の, 雌の 名婦人, 雌

□ **fertilizer** 名①(化学) 肥料 ②豊かにする人[物] ③受精媒介者

□ **fiber** 名①繊維, 食物繊維, 繊維質 ②性格, 性質 ③強さ, 堅牢性

□ **financial** 形①財務(上)の, 金融(上)の ②金融関係者の **illicit financial flows** 違法な資金の流れ

□ **find out** 見つけ出す, 気がつく, 知る, 調べる, 解明する

□ **Finland** 名フィンランド《国名》

□ **firm** 名会社, 事務所 形堅い, しっかりした, 断固とした 副しっかりと

□ **fiscal** 形財務の, 財政上の, 会計の, 国庫の

□ **fishing** 名釣り, 漁業

□ **fit** 動合致[適合]する, 合致させる

□ **fix** 動①固定する[させる] ②修理する ③決定する ④用意する, 整える

□ **flash** 名閃光, きらめき

□ **flash flood** 鉄砲水

□ **floating** 形浮いて[浮遊して]いる

□ **flood** 名①洪水 ②殺到 **flash flood** 鉄砲水

□ **flooding** 名洪水, 氾濫

□ **flow** 動流れ出る, 流れる, あふれる 名①流出 ②流ちょう(なこと) **illicit financial flows** 違法な資金の流れ

□ **focus** 名①焦点, ピント ②関心の的, 着眼点 ③中心 動①焦点を合わせる ②(関心・注意を)集中させる

□ **followed by** その後に～が続いて

□ **following** 動follow (ついていく) の現在分詞 形《the –》次の, 次に続く 名《the –》下記のもの, 以下に述べるもの

□ **food aid** 食糧援助[支援]

□ **food drive** フードドライブ《家庭で余っている未開封の食品を持ち寄り, フードバンクや地域の福祉施設などに寄付する活動》

□ **food loss** フードロス《規格外品, キズや腐敗などで食べられなくなったもの, 売れ残った商品など, 生産から販売までの過程で発生する, まだ食べられるのに捨てられる食品》

□ **food mileage** フードマイレージ《食料が消費者に届くまでに輸送される距離を数字で表したもの。食料輸入量に輸出入国首都間の距離を掛けたものを輸入国別に算出・集計して表す》

□ **food shortage** 食糧不足

□ **food waste** フードウェイスト《食べ残し, 賞味期限切れ, 過剰購入による余剰など, 消費者が購入後に捨てられる食品》

□ **footprint** 名足型, 足跡 **carbon footprint** カーボンフットプリント (商品やサービスのライフサイクル全体で排出される温室効果ガスの排出量をCO_2排出量に換算して表示したもの)

□ **for example** たとえば

□ **for instance** たとえば

□ **for oneself** 独力で, 自分のために

□ **force** 图力, 勢い 動①強制する, 力ずくで~する, 余儀なく~させる ②押しやる, 押し込む

□ **forced** 形強制された, 強制的な

□ **forced labor** 強制労働

□ **Forest Stewardship Council** 森林管理協議会《責任ある森林管理を普及させるために設立された国際的な非営利団体》

□ **forested** 形森林に覆われた

□ **form** 图①形, 形式 ②書式

□ **former** 形①前の, 先の, 以前の ②《the –》(二者のうち)前者の

□ **fossil** 图①化石 ②時代遅れの人, 古くさい考え

□ **fossil fuel** 化石燃料《石炭・石油など》

□ **foundation** 图①建設, 創設 ②基礎, 土台

□ **fourth-highest** 形4番目に高い

□ **France** 图フランス《国名》

□ **free school** フリースクール《不登校の子供に対し, 学習活動, 教育相談, 体験活動などの活動を行っている民間の施設》

□ **free trade** 自由貿易

□ **freedom** 图①自由 ②束縛がないこと

□ **freelancer** 图フリーランサー

□ **frequently** 副頻繁に, しばしば

□ **friendly** 形親しみのある, 親切な, 友情のこもった

□ **front** 熟 in front of ~の前に, ~の正面に

□ **fuel** 图燃料 fossil fuel 化石燃料《石炭・石油など》

□ **full-time** 图常勤の, 専任の

□ **fully** 副十分に, 完全に, まるまる

□ **fundraising** 图(慈善団体・政党などの)資金[寄付金]集め

□ **fungi** 图真菌, 菌類《fungusの複数形》

□ **further** 副いっそう遠く, その上に, もっと

□ **furthermore** 副さらに, その上

□ **future** 熟 in the future 将来は

G

□ **gain** 動①得る, 増す ②進歩する, 進む 图①増加, 進歩 ②利益, 得ること, 獲得

□ **gap** 图ギャップ, 隔たり, すき間 education gap 教育格差 gender pay gap 性別による賃金格差 information gap インフォメーション・ギャップ, 情報格差《聞き手と話し手の間にある情報の差のこと》 wage gap 賃金格差

□ **garbage** 图ごみ, くず Pacific Garbage Patch 太平洋ゴミベルト, ゴミの渦《北太平洋の中央にある海洋ごみが多い海域のこと。この海域は, 北太平洋環流によって形成された渦の中に, プラスチックや漁網などの廃棄物が集まっている》

□ **gas** 图ガス, 気体 exhaust gas 排(出)ガス

□ **gasoline-powered** 形ガソリン動力の

□ **gather** 動①集まる, 集める ②生じる, 増す ③推測する

□ **GCED** 略グローバルシティズンシップ教育, 地球市民教育《global citizenship education の略。教育がいかにして世界をより平和的, 包括的で安全な, 持続可能なものにするか, そのために必要な知識, スキル, 価値, 態度を育成していくかを包含する理論的枠組み》

□ **gender** 图(社会的に決められた)性, 性別

□ **gender bias** 性差別, 性差に関する偏見

□ **gender disparities** ジェンダー

格差, 男女間格差

☐ **gender diversity** ジェンダーの多様性

☐ **gender equality** 男女平等, ジェンダーの平等

☐ **gender inequality** 男女不平等, 女性蔑視

☐ **gender pay gap** 性別による賃金格差

☐ **gender-inclusive** 形性差別のない

☐ **general** 形①全体の, 一般の, 普通の ②おおよその ③(職位の)高い, 上級の **in general** 一般に, たいてい

☐ **generally** 副①一般に, だいたい ②たいてい

☐ **generate** 動生み出す, 引き起こす

☐ **generation** 名①同世代の人々 ②一世代 ③発生, 生成

☐ **geothermal** 名地熱エネルギー 形地熱の

☐ **Germany** 名ドイツ《国名》

☐ **get back** 戻る, 帰る

☐ **get into** ～に入る, 入り込む

☐ **get on** (電車などに)乗る, 気が合う

☐ **get rid of** ～を取り除く

☐ **get someone to do** (人)に～させる[してもらう]

☐ **get started** 始める

☐ **get used to** ～になじむ, ～に慣れる

☐ **give birth to** ～を生む

☐ **glacier** 名氷河

☐ **global** 形地球(上)の, 地球規模の, 世界的な, 国際的な

☐ **global citizenship education (GCED)** グローバルシティズンシップ教育, 地球市民教育《教育がいかにして世界をより平和的, 包括的で安全な, 持続可能なものにす

るか, そのために必要な知識, スキル, 価値, 態度を育成していくかを包含する理論的枠組み》

☐ **global partnership** グローバル・パートナーシップ, 世界的提携

☐ **global warming** 地球温暖化

☐ **globalized** 形グローバル化された

☐ **globally** 副グローバルに, 地球規模で

☐ **go** 熟 **go back to** ～に帰る[戻る], ～に遡る, (中断していた作業に)再び取り掛かる **go bad** (飲食物が)腐る **go down** 下に降りる **go into** ～に入る, (仕事)に就く **go up** ①上がる, 高くなる ②上昇する

☐ **good** 熟 **as good as** ～も同然で, ほとんど～ **be not good for** ～に良くない **social good** 社会を良くするもの, ソーシャルグッドなもの

☐ **goods** 名①商品, 品物 ②財産, 所有物

☐ **governance** 名ガバナンス, 企業統治 **Environmental, Social, and Governance ESG** (環境・社会・ガバナンス)《企業の持続可能性を評価する際に使われる3つの基準》

☐ **government** 名政治, 政府, 支配

☐ **grade** 名学年, 等級, グレード, 成績

☐ **graph** 名グラフ, 図表

☐ **grease** 名油脂, 獣脂, グリース

☐ **greasy** 形①油っぽい, 油で汚れた ②脂肪分の多い

☐ **greatly** 副大いに

☐ **green infrastructure** グリーンインフラ《自然の多機能を活用した生活空間の整備や土地利用の考え方》

☐ **greenhouse** 名温室

☐ **greenwashing** 名グリーンウォッシング《環境配慮をしているように見せかけること》

☐ **grey** 形①灰色の ②どんよりした, 憂うつな ③白髪の

□ **grey water**（風呂や洗濯機など）家庭から出る排水

□ **groundwater** 图地下水

□ **grow up** 成長する，大人になる

□ **growing** 形成長期にある，大きくなりつつある

□ **growth** 图成長，発展

□ **GU** 图 GU《日本のファストファッションブランド。トレンドアイテムを低価格で提供している。ユニクロと同じくファーストリテイリングの子会社》

□ **guideline** 图ガイドライン，指針

H

□ **habit** 图習慣，癖，気質

□ **habitat** 图生息地，居住環境

□ **hamburger** 图ハンバーガー

□ **hand** 熟 on the other hand 一方，他方では

□ **hand-in-hand** 副手に手をとって

□ **handle** 動①手を触れる ②操縦する，取り扱う

□ **handwashing** 图手を洗うこと，手指消毒

□ **happiness** 图幸せ，喜び

□ **hard to** ～し難い

□ **harm** 图害，損害，危害 動傷つける，損なう

□ **harmful** 形害を及ぼす，有害な

□ **harvesting** 图収穫 organ harvesting 臓器摘出

□ **hate** 图憎しみ

□ **hate crime** ヘイトクライム，憎悪犯罪

□ **hate speech** 憎悪発言，ヘイトスピーチ

□ **have** 熟 don't have to ～する必要はない have a baby 赤ちゃんを産む

□ **health** 熟 health care 健康保険 制度 mental health メンタルヘルス，心の健康 universal health coverage 国民保険制度

□ **healthcare** 图医療，健康管理

□ **healthily** 副健康で

□ **healthy** 形健康な，健全な，健康によい

□ **hear about** ～について聞く

□ **heat** 图①熱，暑さ ②熱気，熱意，激情 動熱する，暖める

□ **heat wave** 熱波，（長期間の）酷暑，猛暑

□ **heated** 形熱せられた，暖められた

□ **heated swimming pool** 温水水泳［スイミング］プール

□ **heat-related** 形暑さからくる

□ **heat-related illness** 熱中症

□ **heavily** 副①重く，重そうに，ひどく ②多量に

□ **hectare** 图ヘクタール《面積単位。＝1万平方メートル》

□ **height** 图①高さ，身長 ②《the-》絶頂，真っ盛り ③高台，丘

□ **help ～ to ...** ～が…するのを助ける

□ **help ～ with ...** …を～の面で手伝う

□ **help oneself**（困難から抜け出そうと）自助努力する

□ **helpful** 形役に立つ，参考になる

□ **here are ～** こちらは～です。

□ **heritage** 图遺産，相続財産 cultural heritage 文化遺産

□ **hidden** 形隠れた，秘密の

□ **higher-level** 形より高いレベルの，高位レベルの

□ **high-tech** 图（技術の）ハイテク，（最）先端技術

□ **highway** 图幹線道路，ハイウェー，本道

□ **hire** 動雇う，賃借りする 图雇用，

賃借り, 使用料
- □ **hiring** 名雇用
- □ **historical** 形歴史の, 歴史上の, 史実に基づく
- □ **home** 熟 at home 自宅で, 在宅して **smart home** スマートホーム《電気製品などをネットワーク接続によって管理できる住宅》
- □ **honest** 形①正直な, 誠実な, 心からの ②公正な, 感心な
- □ **Hong Kong** 香港《地名》
- □ **hotspot** 名ホットスポット《紛争, 伝染病, 汚染などの危険地点》 **Biodiversity hotspot** 生物多様性ホットスポット《地球規模での生物多様性が高いにもかかわらず, 人類による破壊の危機に瀕している地域》
- □ **household** 形家族の
- □ **housework** 名家事
- □ **housing** 名住宅供給, 住居, 家
- □ **how** 熟 how far どのくらいの距離か how to ～する方法 no matter how どんなに～だろうとも show ～ to ... ～に…のやり方を示す
- □ **however** 接けれども, だが
- □ **huge** 形巨大な, ばく大な
- □ **human rights** 人権
- □ **human trafficking** 人身売買
- □ **hunger** 名飢え, 飢餓 **chronic hunger** 慢性飢餓《貧困や不平等, 農業生産力の低さなどの構造的な問題によって, 長期間にわたって十分な食料を得られない状態》 **sudden hunger** 急性飢餓《災害や紛争などの突発的な事態によって, 食料の供給が途絶えたり, 食料価格が高騰したりして, 短期間に多くの人々が飢える状態》
- □ **hurricane** 名ハリケーン
- □ **hydroelectric** 名水力発電
- □ **hygiene** 名衛生, 清潔

I

- □ **ICT** 略情報通信技術《Information and Communication Technologyの略。インターネットやコンピューターなどの情報技術を使って, 人と人, 人とモノの間で情報や知識を共有する技術》
- □ **ICT education** ICT教育《パソコンやタブレット端末, インターネットなどの情報通信技術を用いた教育手法》
- □ **if** 熟 even if たとえ～でも
- □ **ignore** 動無視する, 怠る
- □ **illegal** 形違法な, 不法な
- □ **illegal immigrant** 不法移民[入国者]
- □ **illegal logging** 違法伐採
- □ **illegally** 副違法に, 不法に
- □ **illicit** 形不法な
- □ **illicit financial flows** 違法な資金の流れ
- □ **illiteracy** 名非識字, 無学
- □ **illiterate** 名読み書きのできない
- □ **illness** 名病気
- □ **illustration** 名①さし絵, イラスト ②図解 ③説明
- □ **immigrant** 名移民, 移住者 **illegal immigrant** 不法移民[入国者]
- □ **immigration** 名①移民局, 入国管理 ②移住, 入植
- □ **impact** 名影響力, 反響, 効果 動①詰め込む ②衝突する
- □ **implement** 名①道具 ②履行 動①実行する ②道具[手段]を提供する
- □ **import** 動輸入する 名輸入, 輸入品
- □ **importance** 名重要性, 大切さ
- □ **improve** 動改善する[させる], 進歩する

□ **improvement** 名改良, 改善

□ **in** 熟 in a way ある意味では, 幾分, ある程度 in addition 加えて, さらに in fact つまり, 実は, 要するに in front of ～の前に, ～の正面に in general 一般に, たいてい in need 必要で, 困って in order to ～するために, ～しようと in other words すなわち, 言い換えれば in particular 特に, とりわけ in place of ～の代わりに in search of ～を探し求めて in terms of ～の言葉で言えば, ～の点から in the case of ～の場合は in the end とうとう, 結局, ついに in the future 将来は in the world 世界で

□ **inadequate** 形不十分な, 不適切な

□ **include** 動含む, 勘定に入れる

□ **included** 形～を含む

□ **including** 前～を含めて, 込みで

□ **inclusion** 名インクルージョン, 多様性の受け入れ

□ **inclusive** 形包括的な, 包摂的な

□ **income** 名収入, 所得, 収益

□ **inconvenient** 形不便な, 不自由な

□ **increase** 動増加[増強]する, 増やす, 増える 名増加(量), 増大

□ **increasing** 形増加する, 拡大する

□ **incredibly** 副信じられないほど, 途方もなく

□ **independent** 形独立した, 自立した

□ **index** 名①索引 ②しるし, 現れ ③指数

□ **India** 名インド《国名》

□ **indigenous** 形原産の, 生まれつきの

□ **indigenous people** 先住民(族)

□ **individual** 形独立した, 個性的な, 個々の 名個体, 個人

□ **Indonesia** 名インドネシア《国名》

□ **indoor** 形室内の, 屋内の

□ **indoors** 副室内で, 屋内で

□ **industrial** 形工業の, 産業の

□ **industrial revolution** 産業革命

□ **industrialization** 名産業化, 工業化 sustainable industrialization 持続可能な産業化

□ **industry** 名産業, 工業

□ **inefficient** 形非能率[効率]的な

□ **inequality** 名①不平等, 不均衡 ②《-ties》起伏, (表面の)荒いこと ③(天候・温度の)変動 ④不等式 gender inequality 男女不平等, 女性蔑視

□ **infect** 動①感染する, 伝染する ②(病気を)移す ③影響を及ぼす

□ **infected** 形感染した

□ **infectious** 形感染性の, 感染力のある

□ **inform** 動①告げる, 知らせる ②密告する

□ **information and communication technology** 情報通信技術

□ **information barrier** 情報の壁

□ **information gap** インフォメーション・ギャップ, 情報格差《聞き手と話し手の間にある 情報の差のこと》

□ **information poor** 情報弱者《情報の入手や利用について困難を抱える人のこと》

□ **infrastructure** 名(社会の)基盤, インフラ green infrastructure グリーンインフラ(自然の多機能を活用した生活空間の整備や土地利用の考え方)

□ **ingredient** 名成分, 原料, 材料

□ **inhale** 動吸い込む, 吸入する

□ **initiative** 名主導権, イニシアチブ

□ **innovation** 图 ①革新, 刷新 ② 新しいもの, 新考案 **technological innovation** 技術革新

□ **insect** 图 虫, 昆虫

□ **install** 動 ①取り付ける ②任命する ③(ソフトなどを)インストールする

□ **instance** 图 ①例 ②場合, 事実 **for instance** たとえば

□ **instead** 副 その代わりに **instead of** 〜の代わりに, 〜をしないで

□ **institution** 图 ①設立, 制定 ②制度, 慣習 ③協会, 公共団体

□ **insurance** 图 保険

□ **intelligence** 图 ①知能 ②情報 **Artificial Intelligence** AI(人工知能)

□ **interest** 熟 **take an interest in** 〜に興味を持つ

□ **interested** 形 興味を持った, 関心のある **be interested in** 〜に興味[関心]がある

□ **internally** 副 ①内部に ②内面的に, 精神的に ③国内に

□ **internally displaced people** 国内(避)難民

□ **international aid** 国際協力

□ **into** 熟 **come into** 〜に入ってくる **look into** ①〜を検討する, 〜を研究する ②〜の中を見る, 〜をのぞき込む

□ **invest** 動 投資する, (金・精力などを)注ぐ

□ **investing** 图 投資

□ **investment** 图 投資, 出資

□ **investor** 图 ①出資者, 投資家 ②授与者

□ **involve** 動 ①含む, 伴う ②巻き込む, かかわらせる

□ **isolated** 動 isolate(隔離する)の過去, 過去分詞 形 隔離した, 孤立した

□ **Israel** 图 イスラエル《国名》

□ **issue** 图 ①問題, 論点 ②発行物 ③出口, 流出

□ **it is 〜 for someone to …** (人)が…するのは〜だ

□ **Italy** 图 イタリア《国名》

□ **item** 图 ①項目, 品目 ②(新聞などの)記事

□ **itself** 代 それ自体, それ自身

J

□ **Japan** 图 日本《国名》

□ **Japanese** 形 日本(人・語)の 图 ①日本人 ②日本語

□ **jeans** 图 ジーンズ, ジーパン

□ **JICA** 略 国際協力機構《Japan International Cooperation Agency の略。独立行政法人国際協力機構法に基づいて設置された独立行政法人。外務省が所管する, 政府開発援助(ODA)の実施機関の一つ》

□ **job-related** 形 仕事に関する[関連する]

□ **join in** 加わる, 参加する

□ **journey** 图 ①(遠い目的地への)旅 ②行程

□ **justice** 图 ①公平, 公正, 正当, 正義 ②司法, 裁判(官)

K

□ **kidnap** 動 誘拐する

□ **kilogram** 图 キログラム

□ **kilometer** 图 キロメートル

□ **kilometer-long** 形 キロメートル長の

□ **kind of** ある程度, いくらか, 〜のようなもの[人]

□ **kindness** 图 親切(な行為), 優しさ

□ **knowledge** 图 知識, 理解, 学問

□ **known as** 《be –》〜として知られている

- □ **known to** 《be –》〜に知られている
- □ **Korea** 图朝鮮, 韓国《国名》**North Korea** 北朝鮮《国名》**South Korea** 韓国《国名》

L

- □ **label** 图標札, ラベル
- □ **labor** 图労働, 骨折り **forced labor** 強制労働
- □ **lack** 图不足, 欠乏
- □ **landfill** 图埋め立て(地), ごみ廃棄場
- □ **landslide** 图地滑り, 山崩れ
- □ **lasting** 形長持ちする, 永続する
- □ **lastly** 副最後に, 結局
- □ **launch** 動①(ロケットなどを)打ち上げる, 発射する ②進水させる ③(事業などを)始める
- □ **lawmaking** 图立法
- □ **layer** 图層, 重ね
- □ **LDC** 略後発開発途上国《least developed country の略》
- □ **lead to** 〜に至る, 〜に通じる, 〜を引き起こす
- □ **leading** 形主要な, 指導的な, 先頭の
- □ **leading cause** 主要因
- □ **learning** 图学問, 学習, 学識 **active learning** アクティブラーニング(能動的学習) **lifelong learning** 生涯学習
- □ **least** 形いちばん小さい, 最も少ない
- □ **least developed country** 後発開発途上国
- □ **leave 〜 for ...** ...を〜のために残しておく
- □ **LED** 略発光ダイオード《light-emitting diode の略》
- □ **led** 動 lead (導く)の過去, 過去分詞

- □ **leftover** 形食べ残しの, 残りの 图《-s》食べ残し, 残飯
- □ **lend** 動貸す, 貸し出す
- □ **less** 形〜より小さい[少ない] 副〜より少なく, 〜ほどでなく
- □ **lessen** 動(物, 事を)少なく[小さく]する, 減らす
- □ **lettuce** 图レタス
- □ **level** 图①水平, 平面 ②水準
- □ **LGBTQ+** 略性的マイノリティ《レズビアン Lesbian, ゲイ Gay, バイセクシャル Bisexual, トランスジェンダー Transgender, クィア Queer[クエスチョニング Questioning], その他 plus》
- □ **life** 熟 **life expectancy** 平均寿命 **Quality of Life** 生活の質
- □ **lifelong** 形終生の, 生涯続く
- □ **lifelong learning** 生涯学習
- □ **lifestyle** 图生活様式, ライフスタイル
- □ **lifestyle diseases** 生活習慣病
- □ **lifetime** 图①一生, 生涯 ②寿命
- □ **lightning** 图電光, 雷, 稲妻
- □ **like** 熟 **feel like** 〜がほしい, 〜したい気がする, 〜のような感じがする **sound like** 〜のように聞こえる
- □ **likely** 副たぶん, おそらく
- □ **limit** 图限界, 《-s》範囲, 境界 動制限[限定]する
- □ **linen** 图①亜麻布, リンネル(類), キャラコ ②下着
- □ **linked** 形結合[連結]された
- □ **list** 图名簿, 目録, 一覧表 **Red List** レッドリスト《ここでは, 国際自然保護連合 (IUCN) が発行する絶滅危惧種のリストを指す》
- □ **liter** 图リットル, リッター
- □ **literacy** 图識字能力
- □ **litter** 图(散らかした)ごみ, がらくた
- □ **live on** 〜を糧として生きる

157

□ **living** 名生計, 生活

□ **living standard** 生活水準 **basic living standards** 基本的生活水準
形①生きている, 現存の ②使用されている ③そっくりの

□ **locally** 副①ある特定の場所[地方]で, 現地的に ②近くで, このあたりで

□ **logging** 名木材の切り出し **illegal logging** 違法伐採

□ **logical** 形論理学の, 論理的な

□ **long** 熟 **as long as** ～する以上は, ～である限りは **long way** はるかに

□ **look for** ～を探す

□ **look into** ①～を検討する, ～を研究する ②～の中を見る, ～をのぞき込む

□ **loop** 名ループ, 輪, 輪状のもの

□ **loss** 名①損失(額・物), 損害, 浪費 ②失敗, 敗北 **food loss** フードロス《規格外品, キズや腐敗などで食べられなくなったもの, 売れ残った商品など, 生産から販売までの過程で発生する, まだ食べられるのに捨てられる食品》

□ **lot of** 《a –》たくさんの～

□ **low-carbon** 形低炭素

□ **lower** 形もっと低い, 下級の, 劣った

□ **low-priced** 形安価の, 低価格帯の

□ **lung** 名肺

M

□ **m** 略メートル《meterの略》

□ **made to** 《be –》～させられる

□ **main** 形主な, 主要な

□ **mainly** 副主に

□ **maintain** 動①維持する ②養う

□ **major** 形大きいほうの, 主な, 一流の

□ **make ~ into** ～を…に仕立てる

□ **make money** お金を儲ける

□ **make progress** 進歩[上達]する, 前進する

□ **make sure** 確かめる, 確認する

□ **make up** ～を構成[形成]する

□ **make use of** ～を利用する, ～を生かす

□ **malaria** 名マラリア

□ **Malawi** 名マラウイ《国名》

□ **male** 形男の, 雄の 名男, 雄

□ **malnourished** 形栄養失調の, 栄養不良の

□ **manage** 動①動かす, うまく処理する ②経営[管理]する, 支配する ③どうにか～する

□ **management** 名①経営, 取り扱い ②運営, 管理(側)

□ **manager** 名経営者, 支配人, 支店長, 部長

□ **mangrove** 名マングローブ

□ **manufacturer** 名製造業者, メーカー

□ **manufacturing** 名製造(業)

□ **many** 熟 **as many as** ～もの数の **so many** 非常に多くの

□ **marine** 形海の, 船舶の, 海運の 名①海兵隊員 ②船舶

□ **marine ecology** 海洋生態学

□ **marriage** 名①結婚(生活・式) ②結合, 融合, (吸収)合併

□ **married** 形結婚した, 既婚の

□ **marry** 動結婚する

□ **mask** 名面, マスク

□ **massive** 形①巨大な, 大量の ②堂々とした

□ **match** 動①～に匹敵する ②調和する, 釣り合う ③(～を…と)勝負させる

□ **material** 名材料, 原料

□ **matter** 熟 **no matter** ～を問わず,

どうでもいい **no matter how** どんなに～であろうとも

□ **measure** 名①寸法, 測定, 計量, 単位 ②程度, 基準

□ **mechanism** 名機構, 仕組み

□ **media** 名メデイア, マスコミ, 媒体 **social media** SNS, ソーシャルメディア

□ **medical** 形①医学の ②内科の

□ **medical care** 医療

□ **medication** 名投薬, 薬による治療

□ **medium-sized** 形Mサイズの, 中型の

□ **meeting** 名集まり, ミーティング, 面会

□ **mental** 形①心の, 精神の ②知能[知性]の

□ **mental health** メンタルヘルス, 心の健康

□ **mentally** 副心で, 精神的に

□ **mess** 名散乱, 失敗, 汚いもの

□ **method** 名①方法, 手段 ②秩序, 体系

□ **microfiber** 名マイクロファイバー, 超極細繊維

□ **microorganism** 名微生物

□ **microplastic** 名マイクロプラスチック《微細なプラスチック粒子》

□ **middle** 名中間, 最中

□ **might** 動《mayの過去》①～かもしれない ②～してもよい, ～できる

□ **migrant** 名移住者, 移民

□ **migrate** 動移住する, 移動する, 回遊する

□ **migration** 名移住

□ **mile** 名①マイル《長さの単位。1,609m》②《-s》かなりの距離

□ **mileage** 名①総マイル数, マイレージ ②マイル当たり料金 **food mileage** フードマイレージ《食料が消費者に届くまでに輸送される距離

を数字で表したもの。食料輸入量に輸出国首都間の距離を掛けたものを輸入国別に算出・集計して表す》

□ **milliliter** 名ミリリットル

□ **millimeter** 名ミリメートル

□ **million** 熟**per million** 100万分の1

□ **mind** 名①心, 精神, 考え ②知性

□ **ministry** 名①《M-》内閣, 省庁 ②大臣の職務 ③牧師の職務

□ **minor** 形①少数の, 小さい[少ない]方の ②重要でない

□ **minority** 名少数派, 少数民族

□ **mitigation** 名緩和, 軽減 **climate change mitigation** 気候変動緩和策

□ **mix** 動①混ざる, 混ぜる ②(～を)一緒にする 名混合(物)

□ **model** 名①模型, 設計図 ②模範

□ **modern** 形現代[近代]の, 現代的な, 最近の

□ **modern slavery** 現代版奴隷《強制労働や人身売買など》

□ **moisture** 名水分, 湿気, 湿度

□ **money** 熟**make money** お金を儲ける **save money** コストを削減する, 貯金する

□ **monoxide** 名一酸化物 **carbon monoxide** 一酸化炭素

□ **monthly** 形月1回の, 毎月の 名月刊誌

□ **more and more** ますます

□ **more than** ～以上

□ **more-efficient** 形より効率的な

□ **mortality** 名①死ぬ運命 ②死亡率, 死亡者数 **child mortality** 小児死亡率

□ **mosquito** 名カ (蚊)

□ **mosquito net** 蚊帳

□ **mostly** 副主として, 多くは, ほとんど

□ **motivated** 形やる気のある

A
B
C
D
E
F
G
H
I
J
K
L
M
N
O
P
Q
R
S
T
U
V
W
X
Y
Z

- □ **motor** 名モーター，発動機
- □ **move around** あちこち移動する
- □ **move away from** ～から遠ざかる
- □ **move in and out** 出入りする
- □ **move to** ～に引っ越す
- □ **movement** 名①動き，運動 ②《-s》行動 ③引っ越し ④変動
- □ **Mozambique** 名モザンビーク《国名》
- □ **much** 熟 as much as ～と同じだけ too much 過度の
- □ **Myanmar** 名ミャンマー《国名》

N

- □ **nation** 名国，国家，《the –》国民
- □ **national** 形国家[国民]の，全国の
- □ **nationality** 名①国籍 ②国民，国家
- □ **native** 形①出生（地）の，自国の ②（～に）固有の，生まれつきの，天然の
- □ **natural disaster** 自然災害，天災
- □ **nature-based solutions** 自然を基盤とした解決策
- □ **necessary** 形必要な，必然の
- □ **need** 熟 in need 必要で，困って
- □ **negative** 形①否定的な，消極的な ②負の，マイナスの，（写真が）ネガの
- □ **neighborhood** 名近所（の人々），付近
- □ **net** 熟 mosquito net 蚊帳
- □ **New Zealand** 名ニュージーランド《国名》
- □ **news** 名報道，ニュース，便り，知らせ
- □ **newspaper** 名新聞（紙）
- □ **NGO** 略非政府組織《non-governmental organization の略。開発，貧困，平和，人道，環境等の地球規模の問題に自発的に取り組む非政府非営利組織を指す》
- □ **Nigeria** 名ナイジェリア，ナイジェリア連邦共和国《国名》
- □ **no matter** ～を問わず，どうでもいい no matter how どんなに～であろうとも
- □ **no one** 誰も［一人も］～ない
- □ **non-binary** 名ノンバイナリー《男性・女性の二者択一におさまらないジェンダー》
- □ **non-biodegradable** 形生（物）分解不可能な，微生物で分解できない
- □ **non-discrimination** 名差別のないこと，無差別
- □ **none** 代（～の）何も［誰も・少しも］…ない
- □ **nonrecyclable** 形リサイクルできない
- □ **normal** 形普通の，平均の，標準的な
- □ **North Africa** 北アフリカ
- □ **North America** 北アメリカ，北米
- □ **North Korea** 北朝鮮
- □ **northern** 形北の，北向きの，北からの
- □ **Norway** 名ノルウェー《国名》
- □ **not ～ but ...** ～ではなくて… not only ～ but also ... ～だけでなく…もまた
- □ **not good for** 《be –》～に良くない
- □ **notebook** 名ノート，手帳
- □ **notice** 動①気づく，認める ②通告する
- □ **now** 熟 right now 今すぐに，たった今
- □ **nowadays** 副このごろは，現在では
- □ **nuisance** 名うるさい人，やっか

い者, 妨害, 迷惑な行為

☐ **number of** 《a-》いくつかの~, 多くの~

☐ **numeracy** 名基本的な計算能力

☐ **nurse** 名①看護師[人] ②乳母

☐ **nurse's room** 保健室

☐ **nursing** 名看病, 育児

☐ **nursing care** 看護, 介護

☐ **nutrient** 名栄養物, 栄養になる食物, 栄養素

☐ **nutrition** 名栄養(物), 栄養摂取

☐ **nutritious** 形栄養のある, 栄養になる

O

☐ **ocean** 熟 open ocean 外洋 ocean acidification 海洋の酸性化 Pacific Ocean 太平洋

☐ **ODA** 略政府開発援助《Official Development Assistanceの略。開発途上国の経済や社会の発展, 国民の福祉向上や民生の安定に協力するために行われる政府または政府の実施機関が提供する資金や技術協力のこと》

☐ **OECD** 略経済協力開発機構《Organisation for Economic Co-operation and Developmentの略》

☐ **of course** もちろん, 当然

☐ **of the time** 当時の, 当節の

☐ **of which** ~の中で

☐ **off** 熟 cut off 切断する, 切り離す

☐ **offense** 名①違反, 犯罪 ②感情を傷つけること, 気にさわること, 不快

☐ **Official Development Assistance** 政府開発援助, ODA《開発途上国の経済や社会の発展, 国民の福祉向上や民生の安定に協力するために行われる政府または政府の実施機関が提供する資金や技術協力のこと》

☐ **offset** 熟 carbon offset 炭素オフセット, カーボンオフセット(炭素ク

レジットを購入することで排出量の一部を相殺すること)

☐ **oil** 名油, 石油

☐ **old-fashioned** 形時代遅れの, 旧式な

☐ **on earth** 地球上で, この世で

☐ **on one's own** 自力で

☐ **on the other hand** 一方, 他方では

☐ **one** 熟 each one 各自 no one 誰も[一人も]~ない one out of every ~人に1人

☐ **one-fifth** 名5分の1

☐ **one's** 熟 do one's part 自分の役割を果たす on one's own 自力で

☐ **oneself** 熟 by oneself 一人で, 自分だけで, 独力で for oneself 独力で, 自分のために help oneself (困難から抜け出そうと)自助努力する

☐ **one-third** 名3分の1

☐ **ongoing** 形進行[継続・持続]している, 現在進行中の

☐ **online** 形オンラインの, ネットワーク上の

☐ **only** 熟 not only ~ but also ... ~だけでなく…もまた

☐ **open ocean** 外洋

☐ **operate** 動①(機械などが)動く, 運転する, 管理する, 操業する ②作用する ③手術する

☐ **operation** 名①操作, 作業, 動作 ②経営, 運営 ③手術 ④作戦, 軍事行動

☐ **opportunity** 名好機, 適当な時期[状況] equal opportunity [雇用の]機会均等

☐ **option** 名選択(の余地), 選択可能物, 選択権

☐ **order** 熟 in order to ~するために, ~しようと

☐ **ordinary** 形①普通の, 通常の ②並の, 平凡な

- **organ** 图 (体の) 器官
- **organ harvesting** 臓器摘出
- **organic** 形 オーガニックな, 有機栽培の
- **organism** 图 有機体, 生物
- **organization** 图 ①組織 (化), 編成, 団体, 機関 ②有機体, 生物
- **other** 熟 in other words すなわち, 言い換えれば on the other hand 一方, 他方では
- **out** 熟 breathe out 息を吐き出す come out 出てくる, 出掛ける, 姿を現す, 発行される find out 見つけ出す, 気がつく, 知る, 調べる, 解明する move in and out 出入りする one out of every ～人に１人 out of ① ～から外へ, ～から抜け出して ②～から作り出して, ～を材料として ③ ～の範囲外に, ～から離れて ④(ある数)の中から out of balance 不均衡 put out 外に出す throw out 放り出す
- **outdoors** 副 戸外で
- **over** 熟 all over the world 世界中に over and over again 何度も繰り返す over time 時間とともに, そのうち
- **overcome** 動 勝つ, 打ち勝つ, 克服する
- **overcrowded** 形 過密な
- **overfishing** 图 魚の乱獲
- **overpopulation** 图 人口増加, 過密居住
- **overweight** 形 太り過ぎの, 重量超過の
- **own** 熟 on one's own 自力で
- **owner** 图 持ち主, オーナー
- **oxygen** 图 酸素

P

- **pace** 图 歩調, 速度
- **pacific** 形 ①平和な, 穏やかな ②

《P-》太平洋の
- **Pacific Garbage Patch** 太平洋ゴミベルト, ゴミの渦《北太平洋の中央にある海洋ごみが多い海域のこと。この海域は, 北太平洋環流によって形成された渦の中に, プラスチックや漁網などの廃棄物が集まっている》
- **Pacific Ocean** 太平洋
- **paid** 形 有給の, 支払い済みの
- **pan** 图 平なべ, フライパン
- **pandemic** 图 パンデミック, (病気が) 世界的に流行している
- **panic** 图 パニック, 恐慌 動 恐慌を引き起こす, うろたえる
- **parent** 图《-s》両親
- **Paris** 图 パリ《フランスの首都》
- **Paris Agreement** パリ協定《2015年の国連気候変動枠組み条約締約国会議 (COP21) で採択, 2016年に発効した気候変動問題に関する国際的な枠組み》
- **part** 熟 do one's part 自分の役割を果たす take part in ～に参加する
- **participate** 動 参加する, 加わる
- **participation** 图 参加, 関与
- **particular** 形 ①特別の ②詳細な in particular 特に, とりわけ
- **particularly** 副 特に, とりわけ
- **partner** 图 配偶者, 仲間, 同僚
- **partnership** 图 提携, 共同経営, パートナーシップ global partnership グローバル・パートナーシップ, 世界的提携
- **past** 形 過去の, この前の 图 過去 (の出来事)《時間・場所》～を過ぎて, ～を越して
- **patch** 图 継ぎはぎ, 継ぎ, 傷当て Pacific Garbage Patch 太平洋ゴミベルト, ゴミの渦《北太平洋の中央にある海洋ごみが多い海域のこと。この海域は, 北太平洋環流によって形成された渦の中に, プラスチックや漁網などの廃棄物が集まっている》

□ **patient** 形我慢［忍耐］強い, 根気のある 名病人, 患者

□ **pattern** 名①柄, 型, 模様 ②手本, 模範

□ **paved** 形舗装された

□ **pay** 動①支払う, 払う, 報いる, 償う ②割に合う, ペイする 名給料, 報い **gender pay gap** 性別による賃金格差

□ **peaceful** 形平和な, 穏やかな

□ **penalty** 名刑罰, 罰, ペナルティー

□ **pension** 名①年金, 恩給 ②下宿屋, ペンション 動年金を支給する

□ **people** 熟 indigenous people 先住民（族） internally displaced people 国内（避）難民

□ **per** 前~につき, ~ごとに per million 100万分の1

□ **percentage** 名パーセンテージ, 割合, 比率

□ **perception** 名認識, 知覚（力）, 認知, 理解（力）

□ **period** 名①期, 期間, 時代 ②ピリオド, 終わり

□ **permaculture** 名持続型農業, パーマカルチャー

□ **persecution** 名迫害, 虐待

□ **person** 熟 internally displaced person 国内避難民

□ **persona** 名人格

□ **pest** 名（農作物などに対する）害虫

□ **Philippines** 名フィリピン《国名》

□ **photosynthesis** 名光合成

□ **phrase** 名句, 慣用句, 名言

□ **physical** 形①物質の, 物理学の, 自然科学の ②身体の, 肉体の

□ **physical barrier** 物理的な壁

□ **physically** 副①自然法則上, 物理的に ②肉体的に, 身体的に

□ **pick up** 拾い上げる

□ **pie chart** 円グラフ, 分円図

□ **place** 熟 in place of ~の代わりに take place 行われる, 起こる

□ **plan to do** ~するつもりである

□ **planning** 名立案, 開発計画

□ **plastic bit** 小さなプラスチック片, マイクロプラスチック

□ **plastic waste** プラスチック廃棄物

□ **player** 名①競技者, 選手, 演奏者, 俳優 ②演奏装置

□ **pleasant** 形①（物事が）楽しい, 心地よい ②快活な, 愛想のよい

□ **poisoning** 名中毒

□ **policy** 名①政策, 方針, 手段 ②保険証券

□ **polio** 名脊髄性小児麻痺, ポリオ

□ **political** 形①政治の, 政党の ②策略的な

□ **politician** 名政治家, 政略家

□ **politics** 名政治（学）, 政策

□ **pollute** 動汚染する, 汚す

□ **polluted** 形汚染された

□ **polluting** 形汚染する

□ **pollution** 名汚染, 公害 air pollution 空気［大気］汚染

□ **pond** 名池

□ **pool** 名水たまり, プール heated swimming pool 温水水泳［スイミング］プール

□ **poor** 熟 information poor 情報弱者《情報の入手や利用について困難を抱える人のこと》

□ **popularity** 名人気, 流行

□ **population** 名人口, 住民（数）

□ **port** 名港, 港町, 空港

□ **pose** 名①姿勢, 態度, ポーズ ②気取った様子 動①ポーズをとる［とらせる］②気取る, 見せかける ③引き起こす

□ **positive** 形①前向きな, 肯定的な, 好意的な ②明確な, 明白な, 確信し

ている ③プラスの

□ **possible** 形①可能な ②ありうる,起こりうる **as ～ as possible** できるだけ～

□ **potable** 形飲料に適した

□ **potential** 形可能性がある,潜在的な 名可能性,潜在能力

□ **pour** 動①注ぐ,浴びせる ②流れ出る,流れ込む ③ざあざあ降る

□ **poverty** 名貧乏,貧困,欠乏,不足 **absolute poverty** 絶対的貧困 **relative poverty** 相対的貧困

□ **poverty cycle** 貧困の循環

□ **prefecture** 名県,府

□ **prefer** 動（～のほうを）好む,（～のほうが）よいと思う

□ **pregnancy** 名妊娠

□ **prejudice** 名偏見,先入観

□ **prepare for** ～の準備をする

□ **prepared** 形準備［用意］のできた

□ **preservation** 名保護,保存

□ **preserve** 動保護する,保存する

□ **president** 名①大統領 ②社長,学長,頭取

□ **prevent** 動～を防ぐ,抑える

□ **prevention** 名防止,予防

□ **price** 名①値段,代価 ②《-s》物価,相場

□ **priced** 形価格の付けられた

□ **primary** 形第一の,主要な,最初の,初期の 名①第一のこと ②予備選挙

□ **principle** 名①原理,原則 ②道義,正道

□ **probably** 副たぶん,あるいは

□ **process** 名①過程,経過,進行 ②手順,方法,製法,加工

□ **processor** 名①処理装置,プロセッサー ②加工［処理］業者

□ **producer** 名①プロデューサー,製作者,生産者

□ **product** 名①製品,産物 ②成果,

結果 **recycled product** リサイクル［再生利用］製品 **refillable product** 詰め替え用製品

□ **production** 名製造,生産

□ **productive** 形生産性の高い,多くの利益を生む

□ **productivity** 名生産性,生産力

□ **progress** 名①進歩,前進 ②成り行き,経過 **make progress** 進歩［上達］する,前進する

□ **project** 名①計画,プロジェクト ②研究課題

□ **promote** 動促進する,昇進［昇級］させる

□ **proper** 形①適した,適切な,正しい ②固有の

□ **properly** 副適切に,きっちりと

□ **protection** 名保護,保護するもの［人］ **social protection** 社会的保護

□ **protein** 名タンパク質,プロテイン

□ **protest** 動①主張［断言］する ②抗議する,反対する 名抗議（書）,不服

□ **provide** 動①供給する,用意する,（～に）備える ②規定する

□ **public** 形公の,公開の

□ **public transportation systems** 公共輸送［交通］機関

□ **punishment** 名①罰,処罰 ②罰を受けること

□ **put ～ into ...** ～を…の状態にする,～を…に突っ込む

□ **put in** ～の中に入れる

□ **put out** 外に出す

Q

□ **QOL** 略生活の質《Quality of Life の略》

□ **quality** 名①質,性質,品質 ②特性 ③良質

□ **Quality of Life** 生活の質

□ **quantity** 名 ①量 ②《-ties》多量, たくさん

□ **quickly** 副 敏速に, 急いで

R

□ **race** 名 人種

□ **racial** 形 人種の, 民族の

□ **racism** 名 人種差別

□ **railroad** 名 鉄道, 路線

□ **rain** 名 acid rain 酸性雨

□ **rainforest** 名 熱帯雨林 Amazon rainforest アマゾンの熱帯雨林

□ **rainwater** 名 雨水

□ **raise** 動 ①上げる, 高める ②起こす ③~を育てる ④(資金を)調達する

□ **ramp** 名 斜面, 傾斜台, 傾斜路

□ **range** 名 列, 連なり, 範囲 動 ①並ぶ, 並べる ②およぶ

□ **rank** 動 ①並ぶ, 並べる ②分類する

□ **ranking** 名 ランキング, 階級, 位

□ **rate** 名 ①割合, 率 ②相場, 料金 動 ①見積もる, 評価する[される] ②等級をつける

□ **rather** 副 ①むしろ, かえって ②かなり, いくぶん, やや ③それどころか逆に rather than ~よりむしろ

□ **reality** 名 現実, 実在, 真実(性)

□ **reasonably** 副 分別よく, 賢明に, 適当に

□ **recent** 形 近ごろの, 近代の

□ **recognize** 動 認める, 認識[承認]する

□ **record** 名 記録, 登録, 履歴

□ **recover** 動 ①取り戻す, ばん回する ②回復する

□ **recruit** 動 (人材を)募集する, 勧誘する 名 新兵, 新入生, 新入社員

□ **recycle** 動 再生利用する, 再循環させる

□ **recycled** 形 リサイクル[再生利用]した

□ **recycled product** リサイクル[再生利用]製品

□ **recycling** 名 リサイクリング, 再生利用

□ **Red List** レッドリスト《ここでは, 国際自然保護連合 (IUCN) が発行する絶滅危惧種のリストを指す》

□ **redistribute** 動 再び配分する

□ **redistribution** 名 再分配

□ **redistribution of wealth** 富の再分配

□ **reduce** 動 ①減じる ②しいて~させる, (~の)状態にする

□ **reef** 名 暗礁, 岩礁 coral reef サンゴ礁

□ **refer** 動 ①《-to~》~に言及する, ~と呼ぶ ②~を参照する, ~に問い合わせる

□ **refillable** 形 詰め替え可能な

□ **refillable product** 詰め替え用製品

□ **reforestation** 名 森林再生

□ **refugee** 名 難民, 避難者, 亡命者 climate change refugee 気候変動避難民《気候変動や, それによる災害で避難を余儀なくされた人々》 refugee camp 難民キャンプ, 難民収容所

□ **regarding** 前 ~に関しては, ~について

□ **region** 名 ①地方, 地域 ②範囲

□ **regular** 形 ①規則的な, 秩序のある ②定期的な, 一定の, 習慣的

□ **related** 形 ①関係のある, 関連した ②姻戚の

□ **relationship** 名 関係, 関連, 血縁関係

□ **relative** 形 関係のある, 相対的な 名 親戚, 同族

□ **relative poverty** 相対的貧困

□ **release** 動解き放す, 釈放する

□ **reliable** 形信頼できる, 確かな

□ **relieve** 動 (心配・苦痛などを) 軽減する, ほっとさせる

□ **religion** 名宗教, 〜教, 信条

□ **religious** 形①宗教の ②信心深い

□ **rely** 動 (人が…に) 頼る, 当てにする

□ **remain** 動①残っている, 残る ②(〜の) ままである [いる]

□ **remaining** 形残った, 残りの

□ **remote** 形①(距離・時間的に) 遠い, 遠隔の ②人里離れた ③よそよそしい

□ **renewable** 形更新 [回復] できる

□ **renewable energy** 再生可能エネルギー

□ **repair** 動修理 [修繕] する

□ **repeatedly** 副繰り返して, たびたび

□ **replace** 動①取り替える, 差し替える ②元に戻す

□ **require** 動①必要とする, 要する ②命じる, 請求する

□ **research** 名調査, 研究

□ **researcher** 名調査員, 研究者

□ **reserves** 名 (自然) 保護区

□ **resident** 名居住者, 在住者

□ **resilience** 名回復力, 復元力

□ **resilient** 形回復力のある, 立ち直りが早い

□ **resource** 名資源, 天然資源

□ **respect** 名①尊敬, 尊重 ②注意, 考慮

□ **responsibility** 名①責任, 義務, 義理 ②負担, 責務

□ **responsible** 形責任のある, 信頼できる, 確実な

□ **responsibly** 副責任をもって, 確かに

□ **restoration** 名回復, 復活, 修復

ecological [nature] restoration 生態 [自然] 回復

□ **restore** 動元に戻す, 復活させる

□ **restroom** 名 (デパート・レストラン・映画館などの) 化粧室, 洗面所, トイレ

□ **result** 名結果, 成り行き, 成績 **as a result** その結果 (として) **as a result of** 〜の結果 (として)

□ **retailer** 名小売り業者, 小売り商売をする人, 小売り店

□ **retire** 動引き下がる, 退職 [引退] する

□ **return to** 〜に戻る, 〜に帰る

□ **reusable** 形再利用 [再使用] できる

□ **reuse** 名再使用, 再利用, リユース

□ **revolution** 名①革命, 変革 ②回転, 旋回 **industrial revolution** 産業革命

□ **rid** 動取り除く **get rid of** 〜を取り除く

□ **ride** 熟 **sharing ride** ライドシェア 《自家用車を他の人と共有して移動する移動手段》

□ **right now** 今すぐに, たった今

□ **rights** 熟 **human rights** 人権

□ **risk** 名危険

□ **robot** 名ロボット

□ **role** 名①(劇などの) 役 ②役割, 任務

□ **roll** 動①転がる, 転がす ②(波などが) うねる, 横揺れする ③(時が) たつ

□ **room** 熟 **nurse's room** 保健室

□ **rooted** 形根付いた, 定着した

□ **run in** 流し込む

□ **rural** 形田舎の, 地方の

□ **rural depopulation** 農村部の人口減少

□ **Russia** 名ロシア《国名》

166

S

☐ **sadly** 副 悲しそうに，不幸にも

☐ **safely** 副 安全に，間違いなく

☐ **safety** 名 安全，無事，確実

☐ **salary** 名 給料

☐ **sale** 名 販売，取引，大売り出し

☐ **same ~ as ...**《the –》…と同じ（ような）~

☐ **sanitation** 名 公衆衛生

☐ **Saudi Arabia** サウジアラビア《国名》

☐ **save** 動 節約する，蓄える

☐ **save money** コストを削減する，貯金する

☐ **saying** 名 ことわざ，格言，発言

☐ **school** 熟 **free school** フリースクール《不登校の子供に対し，学習活動，教育相談，体験活動などの活動を行っている民間の施設》**tutoring school** 学習塾

☐ **score** 名 （競技の）得点，スコア，（試験の）点数，成績

☐ **SDG** 略 SDGs（持続可能な開発目標）の単数形

☐ **SDG wedding cake** SDGsウェディングケーキ《気候変動や海洋汚染，貧困問題などの社会問題解決に向けて定められた17の目標を「生物圏（Biosphere）」「社会圏（Society）」「経済圏（Economy）」の3つの層に分類したもの》

☐ **SDGs** 略 持続可能な開発目標《Sustainable Development Goalsの略》

☐ **sea creature** 海の生き物，海獣

☐ **seafood** 名 海産物

☐ **search** 動 捜し求める，調べる 名 捜査，探索，調査 **in search of** ~を探し求めて

☐ **seawater** 名 海水

☐ **sector** 名 ①（産業などの）部門，セクター ②（幾何で）扇形

☐ **security** 名 ①安全(性)，安心 ②担保，抵当，《-ties》有価証券 **water security** 水の安全保障（その国の水資源量や水資源管理において安全な状態を保障すること）

☐ **seem** 動 （~に）見える，（~のように）思われる

☐ **seen as** 《be –》~として見られる

☐ **self-driving** 形 （車などが）自動運転の

☐ **self-driving car** 自動運転車

☐ **senior** 形 年長の，年上の，古参の，上級の 名 年長者，先輩，先任者

☐ **sentence** 名 文

☐ **separated** 形 分離する，分別する

☐ **separation** 名 分離(点)，離脱，分類，別離

☐ **serious** 形 ①まじめな，真剣な ②重大な，深刻な，（病気などが）重い

☐ **service** 名 ①勤務，業務 ②公益事業 ③点検，修理 ④奉仕，貢献

☐ **severe** 形 厳しい，深刻な，激しい

☐ **sewage** 名 汚水，汚物

☐ **sex** 名 性，性別，男女

☐ **sexual** 形 性の，性的な，セクシャルな

☐ **sexual exploitation** 性的搾取

☐ **shade** 名 ①陰，日陰 ②日よけ

☐ **sharing economy** シェアリングエコノミー，共有型経済《個人が保有する物やスキル，サービスをインターネットを介して提供したり共有したりする仕組み》

☐ **sharing ride** ライドシェア《自家用車を他の人と共有して移動する移動手段》

☐ **shellfish** 名 貝，甲殻類《カニ，エビなど》

☐ **shelter** 名 ①避難所，隠れ家 ②保護，避難

☐ **Shizuoka** 名 静岡（県）

A
B
C
D
E
F
G
H
I
J
K
L
M
N
O
P
Q
R
S
T
U
V
W
X
Y
Z

- **shopping** 名買い物
- **shortage** 名不足, 欠乏 **food shortage** 食糧不足 **water shortage** 水不足
- **show ~ how to ...** ~に…のやり方を示す
- **shown** 動 show (見せる) の過去分詞
- **shrimp** 名小エビ, シュリンプ
- **shrink** 動①縮む, 縮小する ②尻込みする, ひるむ
- **shut** 動①閉まる, 閉める, 閉じる ②たたむ ③閉じ込める ④shutの過去, 過去分詞
- **sickness** 名病気
- **sidewalk** 名歩道
- **significant** 形①重要な, 有意義な ②大幅な, 著しい ③意味ありげな
- **significantly** 副大いに, 著しく
- **similar** 形同じような, 類似した, 相似の
- **simultaneously** 副同時に, 一斉に
- **Singapore** 名シンガポール《国名》
- **single** 形①たった1つの ②1人用の, それぞれの ③独身の ④片道の 名①片道乗車券 ②(ホテルなどの)1人用の部屋 ③《-s》(テニスなどの) シングルス
- **single-use** 形使い捨ての
- **sink** 動沈む, 沈める, 落ち込む 名(台所の) 流し
- **situation** 名①場所, 位置 ②状況, 境遇, 立場
- **skill** 名①技能, 技術 ②上手, 熟練
- **slavery** 名奴隷制度, 奴隷状態 **modern slavery** 現代版奴隷(強制労働や人身売買など)
- **slow down** 速度を落とす
- **slow fashion** スローファッション《人権・環境・動物などに配慮した衣料品》
- **slowly** 副遅く, ゆっくり
- **slum** 名《-s》スラム街
- **smart** 形①利口な, 抜け目のない ②きちんとした, 洗練された
- **smart city** スマートシティ《デジタル技術を活用して, 都市インフラ・施設や運営業務等を最適化し, 企業や生活者の利便性・快適性の向上を目指す都市》
- **smart home** スマートホーム《電気製品などをネットワーク接続によって管理できる住宅》
- **smartphone** 名スマートフォン, スマホ
- **smoke** 名煙, 煙状のもの
- **smoking** 名喫煙
- **so** 熟 **and so on** ~など, その他もろもろ **so many** 非常に多くの **so that** ~するために, それで, ~できるように **so ~ that ...** 非常に~なので…
- **so-called** 形いわゆる
- **soccer** 名サッカー
- **social** 形①社会の, 社会的な ②社交的な, 愛想のよい **Environmental, Social, and Governance** ESG《環境・社会・ガバナンス》《企業の持続可能性を評価する際に使われる3つの基準》
- **social good** 社会を良くするもの, ソーシャルグッドなもの
- **social media** SNS, ソーシャルメディア
- **social protection** 社会的保護
- **society** 名社会, 世間 **aging of society** 高齢化社会
- **soil** 名土, 土地
- **solar** 形太陽の, 太陽光線を利用した
- **solar-powered** 形太陽光発電の
- **soldier** 名兵士, 兵卒

WORD LIST

☐ **solution** 名①分解, 溶解 ②解決, 解明, 回答 **nature-based solutions** 自然を基盤とした解決策

☐ **solve** 動解く, 解決する

☐ **Somalia** 名ソマリア《国名》

☐ **someday** 副いつか, そのうち

☐ **someone** 熟 **get someone to do** (人)に〜させる[してもらう] **it is 〜 for someone to …** (人)が…するのは〜だ

☐ **something** 代①ある物, 何か ②いくぶん, 多少

☐ **sometimes** 副時々, 時たま

☐ **somewhere** 副①どこかへ[に] ②いつか, およそ

☐ **soot** 名すす

☐ **sound like** 〜のように聞こえる

☐ **source** 名源, 原因, もと

☐ **South America** 南アメリカ(大陸)

☐ **South Korea** 韓国《国名》

☐ **species** 名種, 種類, 人種 **endangered [threatened] species** 絶滅危惧種 **endangered wildlife species** 絶滅のおそれのある野生生物種

☐ **specify** 動詳細に述べる, 指定する, 明確に述べる

☐ **speech** 熟 **hate speech** 憎悪発言, ヘイトスピーチ

☐ **spoonful** 名スプーン1杯(分)

☐ **square kilometer** 平方キロ

☐ **staff** 名職員, スタッフ

☐ **stage** 名①舞台 ②段階 動上演する

☐ **stand for** 〜を意味する

☐ **standard** 名標準, 規格, 規準 **basic living standards** 基本的生活水準 **living standard** 生活水準

☐ **started** 熟 **get started** 始める

☐ **starve** 動飢えに苦しむ

☐ **state** 名①あり様, 状態 ②国家, (アメリカなどの)州 ③階層, 地位

☐ **stateless** 形国[国籍・市民権]のない

☐ **statelessness** 名無国籍状態

☐ **stay away from** 〜から離れている

☐ **steam** 名蒸気, 湯気 動湯気を立てる

☐ **steel** 名鋼, 鋼鉄(製の物)

☐ **stewardship** 名(他人から預かった資産などの)管理

☐ **stomach** 名①胃, 腹 ②食欲, 欲望, 好み

☐ **storm** 名①嵐, 暴風雨 ②強襲

☐ **stove** 名①レンジ, こんろ ②ストーブ **cooking stove** 料理用コンロ

☐ **strain** 動①緊張させる, ぴんと張る ②曲解する ③無理に曲げる 名①緊張 ②過労, 負担

☐ **stress** 名①圧力 ②ストレス ③強勢 **water stress** 水ストレス(水に関して日常生活に不便を感じる状態)

☐ **stressful** 形ストレスの多い

☐ **strict** 形厳しい, 厳密な

☐ **strongly** 副強く, 頑丈に, 猛烈に, 熱心に

☐ **struggle** 動もがく, 悪戦苦闘する

☐ **style** 名やり方, 流儀, 様式, スタイル

☐ **sub-Saharan** 形サハラ(砂漠)以南の

☐ **substance** 名①物質, 物 ②実質, 中身, 内容

☐ **subtitle** 名①小見出し, 副題, サブタイトル ②《-s》(映画の)字幕, スーパー

☐ **subtitling technology** 字幕技術《映像や音声コンテンツに字幕を自動または手動で追加する技術》

☐ **suburb** 名近郊, 郊外

☐ **successful** 形成功した, うまくい

A
B
C
D
E
F
G
H
I
J
K
L
M
N
O
P
Q
R
S
T
U
V
W
X
Y
Z

169

った

□ **such as** たとえば~，~のような

□ **Sudan** 图 スーダン《国名》

□ **sudden** 厖 突然の，急な

□ **sudden hunger** 急性飢餓《災害や紛争などの突発的な事態によって，食料の供給が途絶えたり，食料価格が高騰したりして，短期間に多くの人々が飢える状態》

□ **suffer** 動 ①（苦痛・損害などを）受ける，こうむる ②（病気に）なる，苦しむ，悩む **suffer from** ~に苦しむ，~に見舞われる

□ **sufficient** 厖 十分な，足りる

□ **suggest** 動 ①提案する ②示唆する

□ **suicide** 图 自殺

□ **suit** 動 ①適合する［させる］②似合う

□ **super-aged** 厖 超高齢化

□ **supermarket** 图 スーパーマーケット

□ **supply** 图 供給（品），給与，補充

□ **support** 動 ①支える，支持する ②養う，援助する 图 ①支え，支持 ②援助，扶養

□ **sure** 圏 **make sure** 確かめる，確認する **to be sure** 確かに，なるほど

□ **surface** 图 ①表面，水面 ②うわべ，外見

□ **surrounding** 图 《-s》周囲の状況，環境

□ **survey** 图 ①概観 ②調査

□ **survive** 動 ①生き残る，存続する，なんとかなる ②長生きする，切り抜ける

□ **Susono** 图 裾野市

□ **sustainability** 图 持続可能性

□ **sustainable** 厖 持続可能な，環境を壊さず利用可能な

□ **sustainable development** 持続可能な開発

□ **Sustainable Development Goals** 持続可能な開発目標

□ **sustainable industrialization** 持続可能な産業化

□ **sustainably** 副 持続的に

□ **Sweden** 图 スウェーデン《国名》

□ **swimming** 图 水泳 **heated swimming pool** 温水水泳［スイミング］プール

□ **symbol** 图 シンボル，象徴

□ **Syria** 图 シリア《国名》

□ **system** 圏 **public transportation systems** 公共輸送［交通］機関

T

□ **tackle** 图 ①（釣り道具などの）道具 ②（ラグビーなどの）タックル 動 ①（問題などに）取り組む ②タックルする

□ **take** 圏 **take an interest in** ~に興味を持つ **take away** ①連れ去る ②取り上げる，奪い去る ③取り除く **take care of** ~の世話をする，~の面倒を見る，~を管理する **take from** ~から引く，選ぶ **take in** 取り入れる，取り込む，（作物・金などを）集める **take into** 手につかむ，中に取り入れる **take part in** ~に参加する **take place** 行われる，起こる

□ **talented** 厖 才能のある，有能な

□ **tank** 图 タンク，戦車

□ **Tanzanian** 图 タンザニア人

□ **tap** 图 ①軽くたたくこと ②蛇口，コック ③盗聴器

□ **tap water** 水道水

□ **target** 图 標的，目的物，対象

□ **tax** 图 ①税 ②重荷，重い負担

□ **teamwork** 图 チームワーク，共同作業

□ **technical** 厖 技術（上）の，工業の，専門の

☐ **technique** 名テクニック, 技術, 手法

☐ **technological** 形技術上の, (科学) 技術の

☐ **technological innovation** 技術革新

☐ **technology** 名テクノロジー, 科学技術 **information and communication technology** 情報通信技術 **subtitling technology** 字幕技術《映像や音声コンテンツに字幕を自動または手動で追加する技術》

☐ **teenage** 形ティーンエイジャーの, 10代の

☐ **temperature** 名温度, 体温

☐ **temporarily** 副一時的に, 仮に, 当面は

☐ **temporary** 形一時的な, 仮の

☐ **tension** 名緊張 (関係), ぴんと張ること

☐ **term** 名①期間, 期限 ②語, 用語 ③《-s》条件 ④《-s》関係, 仲 **in terms of** ～の言葉で言えば, ～の点から

☐ **testing** 名テストすること

☐ **than** 熟 **more than** ～以上 **rather than** ～よりむしろ

☐ **thanks to** ～のおかげで, ～の結果

☐ **that** 熟 **so that** ～するために, それで, ～できるように **so ～ that ...** 非常に～なので…

☐ **therefore** 副したがって, それゆえ, その結果

☐ **these days** このごろ

☐ **think of** ～のことを考える, ～を思いつく, 考え出す

☐ **thinking** 名考えること, 思考

☐ **third country** 第三国

☐ **this way** このように

☐ **those who** ～する人々

☐ **though** 接①～にもかかわらず, ～だが ②たとえ～でも **even**

though ～であるけれども, ～にもかかわらず

☐ **thousands of** 何千という

☐ **threatened** 形絶滅のおそれのある状態の

☐ **threatened species** 絶滅危惧種

☐ **throughout** 前①～中, ～を通じて ②～のいたるところに 副初めから終わりまで, ずっと

☐ **throw away** ～を捨てる；～を無駄に費やす, 浪費する

☐ **throw out** 放り出す

☐ **thrown** 動 throw (投げる) の過去分詞

☐ **time** 熟 **all the time** ずっと, いつも, その間ずっと **at a time** 一度に, 続けざまに **of the time** 当時の, 当節の **over time** 時間とともに, そのうち

☐ **tiny** 形ちっぽけな, とても小さい

☐ **to be sure** 確かに, なるほど

☐ **toilet** 名トイレ, 化粧室

☐ **Tokyo** 名東京《地名》

☐ **Tokyo Dome** 東京ドーム《東京都文京区後楽にあるドーム球場。面積：0.047 km²》

☐ **ton** 名トン《重量・容積単位》

☐ **too much** 過度の

☐ **tool** 名道具, 用具, 工具

☐ **torrential** 形 (雨が) 土砂降りの

☐ **total** 形総計の, 全体の, 完全な 名全体, 合計

☐ **tough** 形堅い, 丈夫な, たくましい, 骨の折れる, 困難な

☐ **towel** 名タオル

☐ **Toyota Motor Corporation** 名トヨタ自動車株式会社

☐ **trade** 名取引, 貿易, 商業 **fair trade** フェアトレード《農産物などを買う際に, 生産者が適切な収入を得られるように適正価格を支払う運動》

171

□ **free trade** 自由貿易 動取引する，貿易する，商売する

□ **tradition** 名伝統，伝説，しきたり

□ **traffic** 名通行，往来，交通(量)，貿易

□ **traffic accident** 交通事故

□ **trafficking** 名トラフィッキング，不正[不法]取引，密売 **human trafficking** 人身売買

□ **trainee** 名(職業・軍事)訓練を受ける人，見習い

□ **training** 名①トレーニング，訓練 ②コンディション，体調 **vocational training** 職業教育

□ **transform** 動①変形[変化]する，変える ②変換する

□ **transformation** 名変化，変換，変容 **digital transformation** デジタル変革，デジタル・トランスフォーメーション《最新のデジタル技術の活用によってさまざまな分野でより便利に進化すること》

□ **transparency** 名透明性

□ **transport** 動輸送[運送]する

□ **transportation** 名交通(機関)，輸送手段 **public transportation systems** 公共輸送[交通]機関

□ **trap** 動わなを仕掛ける，わなで捕らえる

□ **trash** 名①くず，ごみ ②くだらないもの[人]

□ **treat** 動扱う

□ **treatment** 名①取り扱い，待遇 ②治療(法)

□ **treaty** 名条約，協定

□ **tree** 熟**cut down trees** 木を伐採する

□ **tree-planting** 名植樹，植林

□ **triangular** 形①三角(形)の ②三者の

□ **triangular cooperation** 三角協力《開発援助において途上国間の協力に先進国が加わること》

□ **trick** 動だます

□ **tropical** 形熱帯の

□ **truancy** 名(生徒の)ずる休み，無断欠席

□ **truly** 副①全く，本当に，真に ②心から，誠実に

□ **trusted** 形信頼されている，信用がある

□ **turn into** ～に変わる

□ **tutoring** 名個別指導

□ **tutoring school** 学習塾

□ **typhoon** 名台風

□ **typical** 形典型的な，象徴的な

U

□ **UHC** 略国民皆医療保険制度《Universal Health Coverage の略》

□ **Ukrainian** 形ウクライナ人の

□ **ultra-compact** 形超小型の

□ **UN** 略国際連合，国連《United Nations の略》

□ **UN Women** 国連女性機関，国連男女平等・女性の地位向上機関

□ **unable** 形《be－to ～》～することができない

□ **underdeveloped** 形発展の遅れた，低開発の

□ **underemployed** 形潜在失業の，不完全雇用の

□ **underemployment** 名不完全雇用，過少雇用

□ **undergo** 動経験する，被る，耐える

□ **understanding** 名理解，意見の一致，了解

□ **underway** 形航行[進行]中の

□ **unemployment** 名失業(状態)

□ **unequal** 形同等でない，同じでない

□ **UNESCO** 略国際連合教育科学

文化機関, ユネスコ《United Nations Educational, Scientific and Cultural Organization の略》

☐ **unexpected** 形思いがけない, 予期しない

☐ **unfair** 形不公平な, 不当な

☐ **unfortunately** 副不幸にも, 運悪く

☐ **unhappy** 形不運な, 不幸な

☐ **UNICEF** 略ユニセフ, 国連児童基金《発展途上国の子どもの生活, 保健衛生, 教育の向上を目指す国連の常設機関。United Nations Children's Fund の略》

☐ **UNIQLO** 略ユニクロ《日本のアパレルブランド。実用 (カジュアル) 衣料品の製造小売を一括して展開する, 日本におけるファストファッションの代表的存在。ファーストリテイリングの完全子会社》

☐ **united** 形団結した, まとまった, 連合した

☐ **United Nations (UN)** 国際連合, 国連

☐ **United States** (アメリカ) 合衆国

☐ **universal** 形①全体の, 全世界の②普遍的な

☐ **Universal Health Coverage (UHC)** 国民皆医療保険制度

☐ **university** 名 (総合) 大学

☐ **unlimited** 形無限の, 果てしない

☐ **unpaid** 形①未払いの, 未納の②無給の

☐ **unsafe** 形危険な, 安全でない

☐ **unsustainable** 形持続不可能な

☐ **up** 熟come up with ~に追いつく, ~を思いつく, 考え出す, 見つけ出す end up 結局~になる go up ①上がる, 高くなる ②上昇する grow up 成長する, 大人になる make up ~を構成 [形成] する pick up 拾い上げる use up ~を使い果たす

☐ **update** 動最新にする, アップデートする 名最新情報, 最新のもの

☐ **urban** 形都会の, 都市の

☐ **urban congestion** 都市過密化

☐ **urbanization** 名都市化 (現象)

☐ **urgently** 副緊急に, しきりに

☐ **usable** 形使用可能な, 有効な, 使いものになる

☐ **use** 熟make use of ~を利用する, ~を生かす use up ~を使い果たす

☐ **used** 動①use (使う) の過去, 過去分詞 ②《 - to》よく~したものだ, 以前は~であった 形①慣れている, 《get [become] - to》~に慣れてくる②使われた, 中古の

V

☐ **vaccinated** 形ワクチン [予防] 接種を受けた

☐ **vaccination** 名ワクチン接種, 予防接種

☐ **vaccine** 名ワクチン

☐ **value** 名価値, 値打ち, 価格 動評価する, 値をつける, 大切にする

☐ **vapor** 名①蒸気, 湯気 ②気体

☐ **variety** 名①変化, 多様性, 寄せ集め ②種類

☐ **various** 形変化に富んだ, さまざまの, たくさんの

☐ **vegan** 名ヴィーガン, 完全菜食主義者

☐ **vegetable** 名野菜, 青物

☐ **vehicle** 名乗り物, 車, 車両

☐ **Venezuela** 名ベネズエラ《国名》

☐ **violate** 動 (法など) 破る, 違反する

☐ **violence** 名①暴力, 乱暴 ②激しさ domestic violence ドメスティック・バイオレンス, 家庭内暴力

☐ **virtual** 形①事実上の ②仮想の

☐ **virtual water** バーチャルウォーター, 仮想水《食料を輸入している国

173

において，もしその輸入食料を生産するとしたら，どの程度の水が必要かを推定したもの》

□ **visible** 形 目に見える，明らかな

□ **vocational** 形 職業上の

□ **vocational training** 職業教育

□ **volunteer** 名 志願者，ボランティア 動 自発的に提供する，奉仕活動を行う

□ **vote** 名 投票(権)，票決 動 投票する，投票して決める

□ **voting** 名 選挙，投票

□ **voting right** 投票権，選挙権

□ **vulnerable** 形 弱い，脆弱な

W

□ **wage** 名 賃金，給料，応酬 動 (戦争・闘争などを)行う

□ **wage gap** 賃金格差

□ **waiting** 形 待っている，仕えている

□ **walking** 名 歩行，歩くこと

□ **war** 熟 civil war 内戦，内乱

□ **warming** 名 暖まること，温度上昇 global warming 地球温暖化

□ **waste** 熟 food waste フードウェイスト《食べ残し，賞味期限切れ，過剰購入による余剰など，消費者が購入後に捨てられる食品》plastic waste プラスチック廃棄物 waste disposal 廃棄物処理

□ **wasted** 形 廃棄される，無駄になる

□ **water** 熟 black water (工場やトイレなどから出る)汚水，下水 grey water (風呂や洗濯など)家庭から出る排水 tap water 水道水 virtual water バーチャルウォーター，仮想水《食料を輸入している国において，もしその輸入食料を生産するとしたら，どの程度の水が必要かを推定したもの》

□ **water security** 水の安全保障(その国の水資源量や水資源管理において安全な状態を保障すること)

□ **water shortage** 水不足

□ **water stress** 水ストレス(水に関して日常生活に不便を感じる状態)

□ **water-related** 形 水に関連する

□ **wave** 名 ①波 ②(手などを)振ること heat wave 熱波，(長期間の)酷暑，猛暑

□ **way** 熟 in a way ある意味では，幾分，ある程度 long way はるかに this way このように way of ～する方法 way to ～する方法

□ **wealth** 名 ①富，財産 ②豊富，多量 redistribution of wealth 富の再分配

□ **weather** 熟 extreme weather 異常気象

□ **web** 名 ①クモの巣 ②《the W-》ウェブ(=World Wide Web)

□ **website** 名 ウェブサイト

□ **wedding** 名 結婚式，婚礼 SDG wedding cake SDGsウェディングケーキ《気候変動や海洋汚染，貧困問題などの社会問題解決に向けて定められた17の目標を「生物圏(Biosphere)」「社会圏(Society)」「経済圏(Economy)」の3つの層に分類したもの》

□ **welcoming** 形 (施設・場所・雰囲気などが)快適な，心地良い

□ **welfare** 名 ①福祉 ②福祉手当[事業]，失業手当

□ **well** 熟 as well なお，その上，同様に as well as ～と同様に do well ～がうまくいく，成功する 名 井戸

□ **well-being** 名 福祉，満足できる生活状態

□ **West Asia** 西アジア

□ **wheat** 名 小麦

□ **wheelchair** 名 車いす

□ **where to** どこで～すべきか

- ☐ **whereas** 援 ～であるのに対して［反して］，～である一方
- ☐ **whether** 援 ～かどうか，～かまたは…，～であろうとなかろうと
- ☐ **which** 援 of which ～の中で
- ☐ **who** 援 those who ～する人々
- ☐ **whole** 形 全体の，すべての，完全な，満～，丸～ 名《the ～》全体，全部 as a whole 全体として
- ☐ **wide** 形 幅の広い，広範囲の，幅が～ある 副 広く，大きく開いて
- ☐ **wildlife** 名 野生生物 endangered wildlife species 絶滅のおそれのある野生生物種
- ☐ **wipe** 動 ～をふく，ぬぐう，ふきとる
- ☐ **wisely** 副 賢明に
- ☐ **with** 援 along with ～と一緒に begin with ～で始まる come up with ～に追いつく，～を思いつく，考え出す，見つけ出す help ～ with … …を～の面で手伝う
- ☐ **within** 前 ①～の中［内］に，～の内部に ②～以内で，～を越えないで
- ☐ **word** 援 in other words すなわち，言い換えれば
- ☐ **work** 援 decent work ディーセントワーク（働きがいのある人間らしい仕事）
- ☐ **work in** ～の分野で働く，～に入り込む
- ☐ **work on** ～で働く，～に取り組む，～を説得する，～に効く
- ☐ **worker** 名 仕事をする人，労働者
- ☐ **workforce** 名 労働力，(作業) 要員，従業員総数
- ☐ **working** 形 働く，作業の，実用的な
- ☐ **work-life balance** 仕事と生活の調和，ワーク・ライフ・バランス
- ☐ **workplace** 名 職場，仕事場
- ☐ **world** 援 all over the world 世界中に in the world 世界で

- ☐ **World Fair Trade Organization (WFTO)** 世界フェアトレード連盟《フェアトレードを推奨する各国の組織の連合体》
- ☐ **worldwide** 副 世界中に［で］，世界的に
- ☐ **worse** 形 いっそう悪い，より劣った，よりひどい 副 いっそう悪く
- ☐ **worst** 形《the ～》最も悪い，いちばんひどい
- ☐ **worth** 形 (～の) 価値がある，(～) しがいがある
- ☐ **woven** 動 weave (織る) の過去分詞
- ☐ **Woven City** ウーブン・シティ《トヨタ自動車による，AI (人工知能)，自動運転技術，ロボットなどを導入した実験都市プロジェクト》
- ☐ **WWF** 略 世界自然保護基金《World Wildlife Fund の略》

Y

- ☐ **Yemen** 名 イエメン《国名》
- ☐ **zero-waste** 形 廃棄物ゼロの，ごみゼロの

Z

- ☐ **Zimbabwe** 名 ジンバブエ《国名》
- ☐ **zone** 名 地帯，区域

A
B
C
D
E
F
G
H
I
J
K
L
M
N
O
P
Q
R
S
T
U
V
W
X
Y
Z

English Conversational Ability Test
国際英語会話能力検定

● E-CATとは…
英語が話せるようになるための
テストです。インターネット
ベースで、30分であなたの発
話力をチェックします。

www.ecatexam.com

● iTEP®とは…
世界各国の企業、政府機関、アメリカの大学
300校以上が、英語能力判定テストとして採用。
オンラインによる90分のテストで文法、リー
ディング、リスニング、ライティング、スピー
キングの5技能をスコア化。iTEP®は、留学、就
職、海外赴任などに必要な、世界に通用する英
語力を総合的に評価する画期的なテストです。

www.itepexamjapan.com

ラダーシリーズ
Introduction to SDGs SDGs 入門

2024年 4 月 6 日　第 1 刷発行

著　者　山口 晴代
　　　　エド・ジェイコブ

発行者　浦　晋亮

発行所　**IBC パブリッシング株式会社**
　　　　〒162-0804 東京都新宿区中里町 29 番 3 号
　　　　菱秀神楽坂ビル
　　　　Tel. 03-3513-4511　Fax. 03-3513-4512
　　　　www.ibcpub.co.jp

© IBC Publishing, Inc. 2024

印刷　株式会社シナノパブリッシングプレス
装丁　伊藤 理恵　カバー写真　アフロ　イラスト　テッド高橋

落丁本・乱丁本は、小社宛にお送りください。送料小社負担にてお取り替えいたし
ます。本書の無断複写（コピー）は著作権法上での例外を除き禁じられています。

Printed in Japan
ISBN978-4-7946-0807-9

本書の英文は、山口晴代著『日英対訳 英語で話すSDGs』（2023 年 2 月小社刊）
を元に作成いたしました。